HUNT'S PREFACES
TO PERIODICALS

PREFACES BY LEIGH HUNT

Mainly to His Periodicals

EDITED BY

R. BRIMLEY JOHNSON

Author of *Leigh Hunt: a Critical Biography*; Editor of *Poems by Leigh Hunt*, and *Essays by Leigh Hunt* (Temple Editions); *Essays by Leigh Hunt* (World's Classics)

KENNIKAT PRESS, INC./PORT WASHINGTON, N. Y.

PREFACES BY LEIGH HUNT

Copyright 1927
Reissued in 1967 by Kennikat Press

Library of Congress Catalog Card No: 67-27610

Manufactured in the United States of America

PREFACE

This volume contains, not only the actual Prospectus, Address to Reader, or Preface to each of the newspapers and journals published by Leigh Hunt, but the various articles he inserted, from time to time, in explanation of his objects and methods; to announce some change in price or size of the periodical; or, otherwise, to expound the art of journalism as he considered it should be practised.

These are followed by similar prefatory matter to three volumes which are in substance and tone as truly journals as the rest, though issued in book form. They complete his message to the public as a newspaper man.

R. B. J.

INTRODUCTION

There can be no doubt that, as the first epoch-making step towards the modernising and democratisation of journal-newspapers was taken by Defoe, the second important era of progress was inaugurated by Leigh Hunt.

The inspiration of both reformers was their love for the people. Both introduced features of startling resemblance to many supposed new popular methods of today which were, in neither case, generally accepted or adopted by their contemporaries and immediate successors.

There was, indeed, only a slight touch of the improving or elevating purpose in Defoe's work; but he was a no less earnest and daring defender of the masses he knew so well how to amuse.

Leigh Hunt more openly defied "the Powers," and suffered for his "impertinence." *The Examiner* holds its place of honour in the history of the best Liberal Reform. Though by nature a man of peace who gladly would have passed his life with a book in "slippered ease," Leigh Hunt possessed a political conscience that forced upon

him the rôle of a fighter in the forefront of the
fray. His zeal and his resolution should not be
forgotten; for as a public man he most emphatically "did his bit."

Though not cast in newspaper form, *The Liberal*, in many respects, belongs to the same class
of publication as *The Examiner*, essentially contrasted to the more definitely literary or miscellaneous "Indicators," "Tatlers," and "Journals."

It came into existence as an expression of Reform, the strongest outpost of Liberalism in those
days. Its direct object was to print Byron's extreme attacks on authority, with their blasphemous phrasing, which the noble Lord dare not
offer to his respectable publisher, Mr. Murray;
and for that reason it was edited and prepared in
Italy, where Hunt had been invited to carry out,
with Shelley's welcome assistance, the dangerous
work. It was Shelley's death and the dishonourable withdrawal of Byron (on the private advice
of friends against association with the disreputa-
ble radical, Leigh Hunt) that strangled the project in its cradle. Had Shelley lived, these warn-
ings might very probably have been ignored:
and *The Liberal* might have developed into one
of the most remarkable journals ever issued.

For Leigh Hunt it proved, however, a second

disaster of political effort, only confirming his natural distaste for the arena.

But political writing, however eloquent or philosophic, almost inevitably is doomed to oblivion. The "Leaders" of the past are seldom wisely recalled.

It is the personal, literary, and critical influences of Leigh Hunt upon the development of journalism with which we are here mainly concerned. The Prefaces, Prospectuses, and other personal statements of this volume not only set forth what he aimed at doing for his readers : but they do actually express what he accomplished ; while revealing – with a naive sentimental egoism – the very nature of the man.

We see that in the earlier days of *The Examiner* and its contemporaries he is mainly concerned to prove the general corruption and inefficiency of other papers, the brave and reckless "independence" of young Mr. Hunt. As the years pass and (as we know from outside evidence) the animosity he excited had been nearly softened out of existence, the eager fighter becomes rather parental in his office chair. Everybody, however stupid or illiteral, was now forgiven by this veteran of the press. He will smile and create smiles for those whose thoughts of him are now at once respectful and affectionate. He has won the suffrages of all but the die-hard Tory, and is very much a friend to the whole world; not quite such a "great" man, maybe, as he innocently conceives himself, but a person of importance in his own day, among his own friends.

Now what, in fact, did Leigh Hunt really bring into our newspapers and magazines? There is one word, and one only, to express his contribution, and that is *taste*; not precisely "good taste" in the strict or social sense; to which he at times, no doubt, himself gave just offence.

He encouraged, in every direction, the appreciation of art and the love of beauty. Profounder critics, without exception, made more frequent blunders in critical judgment. His record for "being right" is absolutely unique. No man ever did so much to revive popular liking for Chaucer, the old Ballads, Shakespeare and the Dramatists, and the great names of other lands. No man ever did battle, with finer loyalty and enthusiasm, for the "new men" of his generation – Johnny Keats, apothecary; Percy Shelley, atheist; Byron, profligate; Lamb, drunkard; or Wordsworth, driveller. No man ever moved on, with such open eyes and liberal judgment, to the gospels of his children's children; to welcome Alfred Tennyson as "the Poet" of his critic's "evening hour"; to applaud and explain the hardest of Browning's early works.

We may describe Leigh Hunt's work as sign-post criticism. He did not, indeed, profess to be more than an eager "Indicator" of the honey in books. His theories or reasons for praise, when he troubled to express them, were often enough crude and nearly always sentimental. But he depended far more on copious quotation than learned exposition; he gave his readers the text on which his appreciations were based. And, almost without exception, that text *was* good art, the very food on which the nation's culture and higher thought must ultimately depend.

Missing practically nothing of worth for over fifty years, never submitting to convention or prejudiced authority, and continually carrying back to the finest classics of all ages and all countries, he educated popular thought and taste to the absolutely "best."

Yet assuredly he was neither preacher nor pedagogue. Again and again we read that "pleasure is the object of this journal." He wrote of beauty because he loved beauty; and longed for the world to enjoy it at his side. His enthusiasms were infectious; obviously simple and sincere.

It is extremely doubtful whether any of his numerous journalistic adventures were justified from the financial standpoint. One need not, perhaps, enquire too closely how he contrived to live, marry young, and bring up a large family. No doubt friends were kind.

The aggressive independence of any revenue from advertisements, so triumphantly announced in *The Examiner*, was maintained to the end. This independence cannot be described as a prudent business move. But "business" hardly appears in these pleasant promises and confessions. Yet they reveal, particularly in the airy boastings of *The Tatler*, a quite unconscious instinct for Publicity, which must have produced a good effect on sales. Leigh Hunt, we may be sure, had no direct aim at sales-promotion; but the personal magnetism so naively displayed exhibits a "method" not altogether dissimilar to the psychology of our most progressive copy-writers today.

Here, in fact, Leigh Hunt presents himself to his public with ingenious reiteration. Here, he says in effect, is the mind and heart of a Book-lover, a man of knowledge and thought; most resolutely determined to be a "good fellow," accepted as such. Always before the public, he yet remains a fireside comrade, inviting his readers to a cosy seat in the corner of his book-lined study, or a quiet prowl round his well-filled shelves. "The Indicator," he says, "is my private room, my study, my retreat from public care and criticism, with the reader who chooses to accompany me."

The association between journalism and literature has varied with every age. While the first "news-letters" had little or no pretensions to style, as the fierce party organs of the Civil War were artistic monstrosities, later periodicals were dominated by men of genius like Swift and Arbuthnot, or by the pedestrian magic of Defoe's homely logic and masterly hard hitting; and a later generation were fed on the courtly periods of Addison and Steele.

When the modern newspaper was first evolved, a real organ of news and of party, Lamb was detailed for six-penny jokes, as Coleridge and DeQuincy supplied some criticism or philosophy; but the division between news and letters began with those ponderous expositions of literary authority, *Blackwood*, the *Edinburgh*, and the *Quarterly*, as culture spread to the Athens of the North.

Then, as Defoe had ignored "The Town," to feed and fight for trade and the "Dissenters," Leigh Hunt, in his turn, defied academic dictators, to nourish the man in the street.

As Dr. Johnson had killed the Patron, they maintained, and proved by other methods, that art must ultimately depend upon public suffrage.

Leigh Hunt, indeed, was not a democrat in the modern sense, not actually so democratic as Defoe. For several years he may be said to have acted as amateur Poet Laureate with some distinction, and his enemies always declared that he "loved a lord." In his enumeration of those who "ought to read" *The Tatler*, we may note that he names the "classes" in their conventional "order of precedence." But he is not the only man ready to sacrifice himself for the under dog while respecting "his betters"; and there was nothing of the sycophant or time-server in his admiration of fine clothes and noble mansions. He loved them as objects of beauty, and frankly envied their freedom from sordid worry or toil. He loved no less the cottage and the tramp.

Once more, today, we have *John o' London* and *T. P.'s Weekly*, closely reviving Leigh

Hunt's methods; but he appealed to a wider class than the newly-educated, and members of evening Institutes or the Y. M. C. A.; because, in his day, nearly the whole reading public needed a simple guide to literature, and was entirely ignorant of books not written in their own tongue.

The industry of Leigh Hunt, as a naturally idle man, almost staggers belief. He produced his "Indicators," his best work, as a side line to the practical responsibilities of editing *The Examiner*; he wrote all the daily "Tatlers" for two years; and he was continually putting out anthologies, standard reprints, and volumes about London, besides his critical, poetical, and other original work. Inevitably the material is unequal, much of it definitely second-rate; the marvel is that he maintained as high an average level.

These "Prefaces" may be accepted, as a unique record of a unique achievement. They reflect and expound the bulk of a long life's work, intimately reveal the man, and provide sufficient evidence of the quality of his achievement.

There is, I believe, no parallel example of so much bulk, extending over so many years, of periodical literature exclusively devoted to the service of art and literature, for the direct benefit of the general public, and inspired by the honest desire to give pleasure. In effect, it became a part of the great educational movements that were so closely associated with the liberal progress of the century.

Leigh Hunt was born 19 Oct. 1784 in the "village" of Southgate, and later joined the group of distinguished men educated at Christ Hospital. Though starting life in the War office, he turned to journalism and literature as early as 1808, when *The Examiner* was produced in association with his brother John, the printer, himself an ardent and devoted Liberal with a considerable intellectual equipment. Married in July of the following year, his existence henceforward was, in a sense, uneventful, though domestically unsettled from a financial instability that involved constant moving from house to house.

The two years of imprisonment, 1813-1815, for calling the Prince Regent "a fat Adonis of fifty," and the unfortunate journey to Italy in 1821 – to produce *The Liberal* – were interruptions that, far from stimulating by the breaking up of routine, were probably the direct cause of actual tragedy in his life; though in his later years the general tendency to regard him as a sort of literary patriarch went far to soften the blows of fate.

At this period Carlyle spoke of his conversation as "free, cheery, idly melodious as bird on bough"; and the description would not be inapt for the whole nature of the man and his work. Though the poison Dickens put into Skimpole has long survived the author's indignant denials, there was in fact nothing sinister, selfish, insincere in the childlike and inconsequent charm Leigh Hunt exerted on all his friends. He did not take his troubles lightly at any time, and made constant efforts to conquer a constitutional aversion to business and the practical responsibilities of life.

His latest work, the sixteen papers of "The Occasional," appeared in *The Spectator* from January 15 to August 20, 1859, fifty-four years after his first essay in theatrical criticism; the actual date of his death being August 28, 1859. As Thornton Hunt writes: "Although his bodily powers had been giving way, his most conspicuous qualities — his memory for books, and his affection — remained, and when his hair was white, when his ample chest had grown slender,

when the very proportion of his height had visi-
bly lessened, his step was still ready, and his dark
eyes brightened at every happy expression and at
every thought of kindness. His death was simply
exhaustion : he broke off his work to lie down
and repose."

R. BRIMLEY JOHNSON

London, March 1, 1927

CONTENTS

PREFACES TO
PERIODICALS
BY LEIGH HUNT

_____
℘

THE NEWS

THE CRITIC'S FAREWELL TO HIS READERS

DECEMBER 13, 1807

Saturday Morning

I cannot quit a Paper, in which I have been accustomed to express my most familiar thoughts, without indulging a kind of domestic parting with my Readers. My thoughts indeed, such as they are, will be given to the Public elsewhere, though perhaps with better enlargement; but scribbling habits have their local attachments as strongly as others, and a periodical writer changes his Paper with as much reluctance as a methodic pedestrian alters his Sunday course or a citizen changes the weekly club to which he has contributed his cogitative whiff.

Nor do I conceive that the regret will be entirely on my own side. An author grows upon his Readers like a kind of habitual thinking, and if there be any vanity in supposing that mine will regret me, it is a vanity whose social feelings divest it of half its selfishness. Habit does much for intimacies of every sort: if we reflect on the causes and on the continuance of our various friendships in life, we shall find that half of them, and perhaps the best half, result from long habits of intercourse, from mutual communications of fortune and feeling, that attach more strongly than the finest sensibilities of romance. From these considerations and from what I have experienced during my critical vocation, I may be allowed to hope, that there are among my readers, men of that habitual sociality, men, if I may be allowed the expression, of those fire-side feelings, who will miss my accustomed appearance at the breakfast table. I cannot help fancying one of these newspaper friends bustling down stairs from his chamber to-mor-row morning with slip-shod rapidity, working the cold air all the way between his teeth, and anticipating his parlour blaze, his hissing urn, and his accustomed theatricals: he is in his arm-chair in an instant, gives his fire the ancient and unavoid-able poke, rubs his hands during the usual elevation of the left shoulder, pours out his first cup, and takes his News from the back of another chair: – "*The Critic's Farew* – (reading a few lines to himself) *Ah – well I'm sorry for that*!"

Readers like these will forgive me a little egotism. With six or eight exceptions I have written every theatrical article in this paper from its commencement, and if I have done nothing else, I have certainly proved what was very generally thought impossible, – that a newspaper critic may be impar-tial. Unluckily, however, I have found it necessary to assure my readers, and I do hereby assure them upon my honour, that no consideration ever induced me to speak ill or well of any person connected with the drama, but my duty to litera-ature and to the public; and I assure them also, that in no single criticism, right or wrong, have I ever been influenced by the suggestions of another, except when the judgment of those whose judgment I valued, have strengthened opinions I had *already* formed. Every report to the contrary is the in-vention of ignorance, or vanity, or mere malice. I never re-ceived what I considered as an injury from any theatrical persons; the abuse with which they have spoken of me I re-gard with complacency, because it is the only weapon which they can lift against just criticism, and because it is natural to mankind to impute a severe candour in any thing but its real cause. I know that it would be contemptible and unnat-ural to drink an actor's wine and then to be severe on his genius; I have therefore drunk none of this wine, I have no theatrical acquaintances; I even sacrificed, on the commence-ment of the News, the opportunity of making some very agreeable and perhaps instructive intimacies, because I would have no excuse for wanting the integrity, however I might want the wisdom of a Critic. This is the whole secret of my impartiality. I have lashed folly as strongly as I could, and I mean to lash it as long as I have an eye to mark out and a hand to reach my object; but if ever the whip has touched the heart instead of the head, if ever it has reached the best feelings of human nature, if ever it has lighted upon the wise instead of the foolish, upon the virtuous instead of the depraved, it went beyond my aim, and I sincerely beg pardon of every moral feeling I have offended, of every noble sensibility I have roused. To exercise, however the severest ridicule on bad writers, and especially on those who have occupied the places of good ones, gives no reproof to my coolest reflections, for grave reason is as totally lost upon pertinacious ignorance as the touch of a feather upon an ass's hide. These writers have it always in their power to avoid ridicule by avoiding the stage. If they will thrust their hands into the fire like children, they must expect to be burnt like children, like children to be chastised. Mr. CHERRY, I have understood, is a very good natured and pleasant man, and I rejoice at it with all my heart; Mr. REYNOLDS also is much esteemed, they tell me, by his numerous acquaintance; I rejoice at it with all my heart: but it is really no secret to the world, that honesty and wit do not always accompany each other.

What may become of my contributions to this Paper I cannot foresee: Newspapers are not celebrated for their lasting materials, and it is not every one of its writers who can expect to be rescued from their ruins like GOLDSMITH or JUNIUS. I am prepared to die like the rest of my transitory brethren or to undergo any of the numerous casualties, whether confectionerian, chandlerian, or leather-trunkian, like a true gazetteer. If any of the modern dramatists and myself should meet in a plate of butter, his leaf under the pound and mine over it, I hope we shall smile at each other like two goodnatured sawyers in the same pit, and think of nothing but to do our duty to said butter: — if any young lady should rend me in pieces with her snowy fingers to give her lovely tresses their ensnaring curl, I can only say that I shall be proud to die in her cause. I heartily shake my Readers by the hand and bid them farewell.

☞ 1

---

[1] A sign affixed to many of Leigh Hunt's contributions to periodicals.

THE EXAMINER

A New Sunday Paper upon Politics, Domestic Economy, and Theatricals

1808

Party is the madness of many for the gain of a few. — Swift [1]

PROSPECTUS

The promises of newspapers have become almost as valuable as the promises of courtiers. Every new journal grows vain upon its modest pretensions; the Proprietors, with much unintentional simplicity, are always flattering themselves on their industry and genius; and it must be confessed, that no politics can be more impartial, no criticism more refined, and no general information given with a more literary air, than what these gentlemen intend. But all this is magnificent in its announcement only. The newspaper proves to be like the generality of its species, very mean in its subserviency to the follies of the day, very miserably merry in its puns and its stories, extremely furious in politics, and quite as feeble in criticism. You are invited to a literary conversation, and you find nothing but scandal and common-place. There is a flourish of trumpets, and enter Tom Thumb. There is an earthquake, and a worm is thrown up.

The Reader anticipates us here. "Ay," cries he, "here is the old Prospectus cant: every thing is wretched in comparison

---

[1] Later Leigh Hunt learned that this quotation was from Pope, and a change was made accordingly in the credit line.

with the *New* Paper: we shall have the ancient But in a minute — *But the Proprietors of the Examiner scorn to come forward* — and so forth." This is a very good observation, but a little inapplicable. The Proprietors, who will be the Writers of the EXAMINER, cannot entirely deceive the town, for they are in some degree already known to the Public. *The Gentleman, who has hitherto conducted, and is at present conducting the* THEATRICAL DEPARTMENT *in the* NEWS, will criticise the Theatre in the EXAMINER; and as the Public have allowed the possibility of IMPARTIALITY in that department, we do not see why the same possibility may not be obtained in POLITICS.

The great error of politicians is that old fancy of SOLON, who insisted that it was infamous for a citizen to be of no party, and endeavoured by a law to make the Athenians hypocrites. This conceit not only destroys every idea of mediation between two parties, but does not even suppose that both may be wrong. Yet all history may convince us, that he, who resolutely professes himself attached to any party, is in danger of yielding to every extreme for the mere reputation of his opinion: he will argue for the most manifest errors of this or that statesman, because he has hitherto agreed with him — an obstinacy as stupid, as if a pedestrian were to express his satisfaction with a tempest at night, because he had enjoyed sunshine in the morning.

The big and little Endians in *Gulliver* have not yet taught us the folly of mere party; and one of the most ridiculous inconsistencies in the human character is that enjoyment, which all ages have expressed in satirical productions, without receiving benefit from them: they drink the physic with a bold and pleasant countenance, and instantly prepare to counteract its effect; or rather, every man thinks the physic excellent for everybody but himself. "Party," says SWIFT, "is the madness of many for the gain of a few." When *Scarmentado* in VOL-

TAIRE arrived at Ispahan, he was asked whether he was for black mutton or white mutton: he replied that it was equally indifferent to him, provided it was tender. A wise man knows no party abstracted from its utility, or existing, like a shadow, merely from the opposition of some body. Yet in the present day, we are all so erroneously sociable, that every man, as well as every journal, must belong to some class of politicians; he is either Pittite or Foxite, Windhamite, Wilberforcite, or Burdettite; though at the same time two-thirds of these disturbers of coffee-houses might with as much reason call themselves Hivites or Shunamites, or perhaps Bedlamites.

A crowd is no place for steady observation. The EXAMINER has escaped from the throng and bustle, but he will seat himself by the wayside, and contemplate the moving multitude as they wrangle and wrestle along. He does not mean to be as noisy as the objects of his contemplation, or to abuse them for a bustle which resistance merely increases, or even to take any notice of those mischievous wags who might kick the mud towards him as they drive along: but the more rational part of the multitude will be obliged to him, when he warns them of an approaching shower, or invites them to sit down with him and rest themselves, or advises them to take care of their pockets. As to the language and style in which his advice will be given, it would be ridiculous to promise that which haste or the head-ache might hinder him from performing. Perhaps it must still be left to statesmen to amuse in politics.

With respect to the THEATRIC CRITICISM, the Proprietors merely observe, that it will be in the same spirit of opinion and manner with the *present* theatrical observations in the *News*. The Critic trusts he has already proved in that paper, that he has no respect for error however long established, or for vanity however long endured. He will still admire Mr. KEMBLE when dignified, but by no means when pedantic; he hopes still to be satisfied with Mr. DIBDIN in a Christmas pantomime, but is afraid he shall differ with him as to his powers for comedy. Yet the town may be assured, that if either Mr. DIBDIN or Mr. REYNOLDS should suddenly become a man of wit, the Critic will be as eager to announce the metamorphosis as if it were the discovery of transmuting lead into gold. Perhaps he may be considered vain in proclaiming his qualifications for criticism, but he cannot help betraying how infinitely the dramatists of the day have abused him. He would not have mentioned this, but the natural infirmity of an author, speaking of himself, must be pardoned for once, especially when he does not dwell upon so flattering a subject.

The little attention which newspapers pay to the FINE ARTS, is no little proof of a very indifferent taste, especially when we consider that this country possesses its own school of painting. That we have artists like WEST, who claim every merit so much admired in the old masters except indeed that of being in the grave; and that a youth, named WILKIE, has united HOGARTH with the Dutch school by combining the most delicate character with the most delicate precision of drawing. These great geniuses make us the best compensation for the loss of the drama by reviving Tragedy and Comedy on the canvas. Yet they are scarcely ever noticed except in these annual sketches of the Exhibition, which a newspaper cannot help giving because they constitute part of the fugitive news. We will try therefore to do a little better. An artist will conduct our department of the Fine Arts. If he does not promise for his taste, he promises for his industry. He will be eager in announcing to the public not only the promiscuous merits of exhibitions, but those individual pictures which deserve to engage the public attention singly, those happy rarities, which like the *Wolfe and La Hogue* of WEST, and the

Village Politicians, Blind Fiddler, and *Steward receiving Rent,* of WILKIE, almost create æras in the history of painting.

As it requires but a moderate portion of good sense to regulate the DOMESTIC ECONOMY of a newspaper, the Proprietors might indulge themselves a little more perhaps in promising peculiar care in this department. At any rate they will never acquiesce in those gayer or gloomier follies of the world, whether of rakes or of prize-fighters, to which the papers give their sanction with so cold-blooded an indifference. They do not intend, like the *Society for the Suppression of Vice,* to frighten away the innocent enjoyments of the poor by dressing Religion in a beadle's laced hat and praying heaven to bless the ways of informers; but they will never speak of adultery and seduction with levity, nor affect to value that man, however high his rank or profuse of interest his connection, who dares to take advantage of his elevation in society to trample with gayer disdain on the social duties. As to those selfish and vulgar cowards, whether jockies, who will run a horse to death, or cock-fighters, who sit down to a table on which fowls are served up alive, — as to those miserable ruffians, whether the ornaments of a gaol or the disgracers of a noble house, who thank God for giving them strength by endeavouring to annihilate the strength of others, who, like a Hottentot beauty, value themselves upon a few bones, and call fighting for a few guineas English spirit, they are most probably out of the reach of literary ridicule, which must be read before it is felt: but we shall use our strongest endeavour to hold up them and their admirers to the contempt of others who might mistake their murderous business for manliness. What! Shall English noblemen crowd the highways to admire the exploits of a few thieves and butchers? Shall they rush from the court and the senate to enrich a few sturdy vagabonds with the labour of their virtuous peasantry, to shout over a fallen brute, and to be astonished at that sublime merit which is excelled by the leg of a dray-horse? What an amiable vivacity!

We are almost afraid to say that NO ADVERTISEMENTS WILL BE ADMITTED in the EXAMINER, for this assertion generally means that they will; but the public will be inclined perhaps to believe the Proprietors when they declare, that though they intend to be engaged in the publication of books, they will not advertise a single one of their own works. Advertisements therefore will hardly be inserted for anybody else: they shall neither come staring in the first page at the breakfast-table to deprive the reader of a whole page of entertainment, nor shall they win their silent way into the recesses of the paper under the mask of general paragraph to filch even a few lines: the public shall neither be tempted to listen to somebody in the shape of a wit who turns out to be a lottery-keeper, nor seduced to hear a magnificent oration which finishes by retreating into a peruke or rolling off into a blacking-ball.

If some weekly papers, however, have a page of Advertisements at the beginning, they have also a page of Markets at the end: they commence by informing us of the retail of London, and conclude by communicating the wholesale. This is a pleasant uniformity, especially in a paper containing all the news of the week. But as there are fifteen daily papers that present us with advertisements six days in the week, and as there is perhaps about one person in a hundred, who is pleased to see two or three columns occupied with the mutabilities of cattle and the vicissitudes of leather, the Proprietors of the EXAMINER will have as little to do with bulls and raw hides as with lottery-men and wig-makers.

Above all, the New Paper shall not be disgraced by those abandoned hypocrites, whose greatest quackery is their denial of being quacks. Their vile indecency shall not gloat through the mask of philanthropy, sickness shall not be flattered into incurability, nor debauchery indulged to the last gasp by the promises of instant restoration. If the paper cannot be witty or profound, it shall at least never be profligate.

THE EXAMINER

1808

PREFACE

[At end of Vol. I]

Legislators, lovers, and journalists, are the three divisions of men that most hate to be reminded of their promises. The perjuries of the first are no subject for jesting: the second declare, that Heaven laughs at theirs: and as to the third, I am sure that both Heaven and earth, if the former has any thing to do with the matter, must laugh at theirs. It is with some pride, therefore, that the *Examiner* can close his first volume, not only with a complacent retrospect towards his prospectus, but with the approbation of those subscribers, who, as they were the first to doubt, are now the most willing to trust him.

As the good faith of the prospectus has thus been acknowledged, I need not descant here upon what its promises have already told the public. It will be allowed me, however, for that very reason, while I sketch a slight review of what has been done, to explain what I have attempted without promising: and this consists of two endeavours: first, an humble attempt, exclusive of mere impartiality in great matters, to encourage an unprejudiced spirit of thinking in every respect, or in other words, to revive an universal and *decent philosophy, with truth for its sole object,* and, second, an attempt to improve the style of what is called fugitive writing, by setting an example of, at least, a *diligent respect for the opinion of literary readers.*

I. The community of that petty and prejudiced manner of journal writing, which originated in party-spirit and ignorance united; the proprietors of newspapers, who, with very late exception, have for a long time been divided amongst factions, could in fact procure no men of real spirit, or with the least tincture of philosophy, to manage their publications; or rather their own ignorance and literary corruption never induced them to make the trial; and if these feelings have hurt the style and reputation of newspapers, yet they have prevented true genius from being tempted against its conscience to add lustre to corruption, they have prevented the better part of society, thank God, from being dazzled any longer by political artifice, and they have at length exposed their own worthlessness. The death of two great party-leaders gave a blow to party spirit, of which reasonable men were willing to take every advantage, if the new powers had allowed them; but it now appears that a change of men opposite in opinion is nothing without a change of things opposite in principle. The abuses of the French Revolution threw back many lovers of reform upon prejudices, that were merely good as far as they were opposed to worse: but every prejudice, essentially considered, is bad, is prejudicial; and there must be an end of that uxorious trick of pardoning the corruptions of the constitution for the sake of its benefits, a trick which only those would teach us, who have designs upon its weaknesses.

Mere impartiality, with respect to men, that is, an indifferent repose amidst political bustle, will not teach us to be patriots, though it may hinder us from being placemen. We must shake off all our indolence, whether positive or negative, whether of timidity or of negligence, we must shake off all our prejudices, and look about us; and in this effort we must be assisted by philosophy.

And let us neither be alarmed by the name of philosophy,

because it has been degraded by little men, nor overawed, because it has been rendered arduous by great. Let us regard it in its original and etymological sense, as a love of wisdom, and not in its acquired and ornamental, as an attainment of it. The essence of philosophy is the cultivation of common reason, and as common things are in their nature most useful, though subject to disesteem, and in their perfection most delightful and admirable, so reason is in this respect like the most common of all things, the air, which is liable to so much corruption when shut up and hindered from circulation, but, when suffered to extend abroad, encompasses the whole earth, and is at once the medium of light, and the mover of power. And a freedom from party-spirit supposes in some degree this necessary enlargement of reason; for he that looks continually even on the most brilliant leader of a faction is in as much danger of being unable to see anything else properly, as he that fixes his eye on red, or yellow, or any other brilliant or violent colour; but to look generally on mankind, or on the face of things, leaves the perception as keen and as distinct, as to look on the colour of green, which is the general hue of nature. Freedom from party spirit is nothing but the love of looking abroad upon men and things, and this leads to universality, which is the great study of philosophy, so that the true love of inquiry and the love of one's country move in a circle. This is the "zeal according to knowledge," which I would be an humble instrument of recommending.

II.   The ignorance and corruption of the journals naturally produced a correspondent style. The jarring spirit of past years seemed to have destroyed every political refinement both of speaking and writing. Graceful persuasion forsook the Senate; wit and argument the press. The newspapers, occupied with momentary rumour and invective, appeared to have no leisure for anything becoming; and as the sounds of speech are affected by a deranged constitution, the whole public voice grew vulgar as it grew violent. People are now beginning to change their tone in these matters; but even now, when every other species of literature has gained at least an elegant mediocrity, the progress of periodical style has scarcely reached correctness; and it is remarkable that those papers which are the most politically corrupt, are still the most corrupt in everything else. It becomes a public writer, therefore, to show the company his intellect keeps, and to attempt a language worthy of the sentiments he feels, and the country for which he writes. If a true style consists of "proper words in proper places," the definition is indisputable in political discussion, which ought to be the vehicle of the clearest and purest ideas. What concerns everybody should be universally intelligible, though at the same time it should be written with a care for ornament, and it is for these reasons, that while I have avoided as much as possible the quotation of languages in politics, in order that everybody might be able to read me, I have not hesitated to employ what little pleasantry I could, in order that everybody might wish to read me.

There is very little political writing in the daily papers, and their articles are read throughout, because they are short, as well as of daily and party interest; but I have ever remarked that in the political essays of the weekly prints, the interest of the reader has been proportional to the manner as well as matter of the writing. It is the same in theatrical criticism, a department which none of the papers seems inclined to dispute with a person fond of the subject, the daily ones for want of independence, and the weekly for want of care. I am so immediately before the public in this subject, that I shall say little upon it here. Theatrical criticism has always been a more popular art in France than in this country, and the consequence is that their theatres are twenty times better regulated. The literature with which it is connected allows a more ornamental style than politics; but I would not willingly quote Greek and Latin to the actors, certainly not to the modern dramatists. The treatment of the passions, however, both in actors and dramatists, demands a greater portion of what the schools call Humanity, than any other subject of the day; and I am never so afraid of the criticism of my readers, as when my endeavours to separate the thousand niceties of human feeling may render me liable to the charge of wordiness. But the use of words on such an occasion should be distinguished from their abuse on occasions of simpler analysis. In short, as Theatrical Criticism is the liveliest part of a newspaper, I have endeavoured to correct its usual levity by treating it philosophically; and as Political Writing is the gravest subject, I have attempted to give it a more general interest by handling it good-humouredly. The use of ridicule need not be defended here. As long as there is anything ridiculous, so long will ridicule be proper and even necessary. Who can always be grave, as long as mankind are what they are. Little Miscellaneous Sketches of character and manners have been introduced into the Examiner, as one small method of habituating readers to general ideas of the age. The Fine Arts also have met with an attention proportionable to their influence and national character, as well as to their rapid improvement in this country. Their improvement, indeed, is at once an honour and a disgrace to the nation, for it is the sole work of individuals. *The politicians and the government have not yet acquired the art, which they must acquire, of looking about them with enlarged eyes, and fighting the great enemy with his only good weapon, and his only real glory, the cultivation of the human intellect.*

The Proprietors return their best thanks to their various correspondents, especially to B.F. and H.R., the former for the enquiring and classical spirit with which he relieved the Editor when unable to attend the Theatre, and the latter for an operatical review, which in the present times has been the first criticism of the kind worthy the attention of sound readers.

On their resolution to proceed as they have begun, the proprietors say little. It is in the place where their country is — at the bottom of their hearts.

OF THE EXAMINER

FROM "EXPLANATION AND RETROSPECTION" – THE "EXAMINER" TWENTY YEARS AGO

[*Monthly Repository*, October, 1837]

It was the Robin Hood of its cause, plunder excepted; and by the gaiety of its daring, its love of the green places of poetry, and its sympathy with all who needed sympathy, produced many a brother champion that beat it at its own weapons. Hazlitt, in its pages, first made the public sensible of his great powers. There Keats and Shelley were first made known to the lovers of the beautiful. There Charles Lamb occasionally put forth a piece of criticism, worth twenty of the editor's, though a value was found in those also; and there we had the pleasure of reading the other day one of the earliest addresses to the public of a great man, who, with a hand mighty with justice, has succeeded in lifting up a nation into the equal atmosphere, which all have a right to breathe, — Daniel O'Connell. Let no friend, who ever mentions our having suffered for a "libel" (a word we hate) on the Prince Regent, forget to add, that it was occasioned by the warmth of our sympathy with that nation, and our anger at seeing the Prince break his promises with it.

THE REFLECTOR

A Collection of Essays on Miscellaneous Subjects of Literature and Politics

1810-1812

PROSPECTUS

Of all pieces of fiction, the most amiable and the least interesting are Prospectuses. The reader, who in his love of inquiry, used to catch at every new opportunity of being amused and instructed, has been so often disappointed in this way, that he is prepared to resist every thing in the shape of a promise; and, in fact, the more ardent the promise, the colder becomes his incredulity. In vain the Prospectus comes before him on the most advantageous terms and softest paper: in vain, like the scheme of a lottery, it sets in array its gigantic types to catch his eye, and make him pay for treasures he will never realize: in vain the writer promises him all sorts of intellectual feasts, research the most various and profound, a style the most pithy and accomplished, and poetry, in one word, original. He recognizes the old story; he anticipates at once, in the composition before him, all the beauties of the style, the poetry, and the research: — in short, he crumples up the paper, and forgets the writer as quickly as he does the street-herald, who insinuates into your hand the merits of a pair of boots, or the attracting qualities of a monster.

In presenting, therefore, a new Magazine to the notice of the Public, the Proprietors are not at all inclined, either by their pride or their interest, to take such infallible means of rendering it ridiculous. The RELECTOR will be an attempt to improve upon the general character of Magazines, and all the town knows, that much improvement of this kind may be effected without any great talent. Reform of periodical writing is as much wanted in Magazines, as it formerly was in Reviews, and still is in Newspapers. It is true, there are still to be found some agreeable and instructive articles in the Magazines – a few guineas thrown by richer hands into the poor's box: – indolent genius will now and then contribute a lucky paragraph, and should enquiry have no better place of resort, it will scarcely fail of a *brief* answer from among a host of readers. But the field is either given up to the cultivation of sorry plants, or it is cut up into a petty variety of produce to which every thing important is sacrificed. It is needless to descant on the common lumber that occupies the greater portion of these publications – on the want of original discussion; or the recipes for and against cooking and coughing; or the stale jests; or the plagiarisms; or the blinking pettiness of antiquarianism, which goes toiling like a mole under every species of rubbish, and sees no object so stupendous as an old house or a belfry; or lastly, on the quarrels between Verax and Philalethes, who fight for months together upon a straw, and prove at last, to the great edification of the reader, that neither is to be believed. – The old Magazines are notoriously in their dotage; and as to the new ones, that have lately appeared, they have returned to the infancy of their species – to pattern-drawing, doll-dressing, and a song about Phillis. These flimsy publications, though unworthy of notice in themselves, are injurious to the taste of the town in more than one respect, inasmuch as they make *a show of employing the Arts*, while they are only degrading and wasting them. Their principal feature is *superb embellishment*, otherwise called *unique, splendid*, and *unrivalled*; that is to say, two or three coloured plates of fine ladies and fashions, hastily tricked up by some unfortunate engraver, who, from want of a better taste in the country, is compelled to throw away his time and talents upon these gorgeous nothings. To suit the style of the ornamental part, the literary presents you with a little fashionable biography; some remarks at length on eating, drinking or dressing; an anecdote or two; a design or two for handkerchiefs and settees; a country-dance; a touch of botany, a touch of politics, a touch of criticism; a faux pas; and a story *to be continued*, like those of the Improvisatori, who throw down their hats at an interesting point and must be paid more to proceed. The *original poetry* need not be described: of all the antiquities of a Magazine, this is the most antique, – a continual round of sad hours, of lips, darts, and epitaphs, of sighings *Ah why!* and wonderings *Ah where!*

It is thus, that in the best as well as worst Magazines, you see a multiplicity of trifles taking place of all that is most important in the *character of the times* – that character, which, as it is the most useful feature, ought also to be the most prominent and most engaging feature in this species of publication. A Magazine should properly be a *Chronicle for posterity*, but what will posterity care for our queries upon wooden legs, and our squabbles upon a turnip? And what will it think of the intellect of an age, which in the midst of so many and such mighty interests could be content with a trifling so frivolous?

These are faults easily avoided by such as have the least regard for the age and its reputation; and to avoid the grosser faults of Magazines will be the first aim, perhaps the best recommendation, of the REFLECTOR. – One of its first cares will be *Politics*, which the Magazines generally dismiss in crude and impatient sketches. Politics, in times like these, should naturally take the lead in periodical discussion, because they have an importance and interest almost unexampled in history, and because *they are now, in their turn, exhibiting their re-action upon literature, as literature in the preceding age exhibited its action upon them.* People, fond of books, and of the gentler arts of peace, are very apt to turn away from politics as from a barren and fearful ground, productive of nothing but blood-stained laurels; they see there, no doubt, the traces of the greatest misery and folly; but if they look a little more narrowly, they will see also the seeds of the most flourishing and refreshing arts. What such men neglect from distaste, less minds neglect from regarding politics in too common, too every-day a light, and in our own age, we have seen a whole nation, which has been called "thinking," gradually lose the habit of looking out upon the times at large, because it has been occupied with a thousand petty squabbles and interests. This is a fault, which as it is one of the most fatal to political character, a writer should be most earnest to deprecate. It becomes us all to philosophize as much as possible in an age, when *human intellect*, opposed to *human weakness*, has been called so unobstructedly into play, and has risen so fearfully into power. Each number of the REFLECTOR will contain, besides a Retrospect of the Quarterly Events, an Essay or two upon Domestic or Foreign Policy; and in ascending from particulars to generals, it will endeavour to view the times in that *historical* light, which striking in broad and centrical masses, and not wasting itself on the corners and detail of the picture, gives prominence, clearness, and effect to the principal objects. Its opinions will be exactly those of the *Examiner*, speaking freely of all parties without exception, attached most strongly to the Constitution in letter and in spirit, and for that single reason most anxious for Reform. The Editor speaks of his independence in this matter without fear of rebuff, not only because he knows not a single politician personally, and is conscious of having as undisturbed opinions on the subject as he has upon the theatre or the weather, but because the readers of the *Examiner* have acknowledged the consistency of that paper, and he has had the good fortune to make the most infamous writers in town his enemies. The only piece of interest he shall solicit for the RE-FLECTOR, is to recommend it to those gentlemen as a work, which he trusts will be worthy of their unqualified abuse and most ferocious patronage.

In *Theatrical Criticism*, the Magazines, generally speaking, have always been the unambitious and unthinking followers of the Daily Papers; and personal interest is of so active and social a disposition that it always finds means to corrupt a trading spirit, equally petty in its views of reputation. It is true, the Newspapers themselves at last begin to be ashamed of praising writers, who have become bye-words for nonsense, and they dismiss the subject, if not with their former panegyrics, with a flippant indulgence half-ashamed of itself. But this style is utterly unworthy of a subject so important to the manners and literary character of a nation, and serves no purpose but to expose the critic and make the very dramatists despise him. The Editor of the REFLECTOR, occupied in another work with exposing the grinning monsters that are every day given to the world as representations of nature, does not intend to particularize so much in the Magazine: – he will do his best to review the quarterly theatricals in their general character, with less of minute, but more of comparative and didactic criticism. The theatres, in their proper state, afford a most instructive as well as amusing course of lessons to a cultivated nation, not, as their enemies insinuate, because they pretend to teach morals better than religion itself, but because they exhibit our virtues in social action and instruct us in that kind of wisdom, which, without being worldly-minded, is so adapted to keep us in proper harmony with the world. But occupied as they have been for years past with mere caricature, they obtain neither the social nor the sentimental end of the drama, they shew us neither what we are nor what we ought to be. A person, wishing to be profited by modern comedy, might amuse and edify himself just as well by making all sorts of faces in a looking-glass. When SHAKSPEARE appears now and then in the list of performances, he looks like a sage in a procession of merry-andrews, and is suffered to pass by with little more than a cold respect. He carries too great an air of truth, and does not make people laugh enough. This is the more to be lamented, since a taste for the drama is never so easily and entirely vitiated, as when self-love is left undisturbed to its frivolous enjoyments, when advice thinks only how it shall appear ridiculous, and satire grows powerless from neglecting its real objects. The better part of the town have acquired sense enough to despise these things, critically speaking, but if they still continue to be amused by them, they will only be despised in their turn, as one of the dramatists plainly hinted the other day in a preface. You may hold a fool in a contemptible light, but when you condescend to laugh and be on a level with him, he is more than even with your contempt.

The *Fine Arts* are in a very different state from the Drama, and demand a different mode of treatment. The latter is in its second infancy with all the vices of a frivolous dotage, and must, if possible, be ground young again: – the former are in their first infancy and must be handled more tenderly, though at the same time with no vicious indulgence. The Proprietors need not descant on the want of all ardour upon this head in our periodical works. It is said that the country at present has no notion of a taste for art; and WINCKELMANN, who from continually contemplating the southern sunshine, seems to have looked upon us with spots before his eyes, said that it always did and always would want a taste, from the nature of its climate. He forgot that our poets have never been surpassed; that Paris, which was the focus of literary taste, is in the same latitude with Tartary; and that Athens is situate beneath a fickle sky. There are, no doubt, several obstructions in the way of modern art, and among them, however trivial it may appear at first sight, the constrained and concealing style of modern dress is a formidable hindrance to the attainment of a noble and familiar mastery of form. But these disadvantages have become common to all Europe. A fine climate, an enlivening sunshine, an atmosphere, free and lucid, through which objects become pictures, may certainly dispose the mind to its own enjoyment, and the fancy to an undisturbed leisure of creation; and from this circumstance it is likely, that taste and a love of genius will be more *diffused* among warm countries than others. But there are minds that are above all circumstances of this kind in regard to genius, and there will be always a sufficient number of such minds in an *intellectual nation*, if they exert themselves as they ought, and call forth the public attention. It is *government* – not easy or happy government in particular, but government of a disposition to patronize, or of a nature to rouse emulation, that has the greatest influence in these matters. In fact, how came WINCKELMANN himself, a Prussian by birth and education, to be the most enthusiastic, some say the best, connoisseur of his time? Or how is it that Flanders has produced better painters than all the south of Europe, Italy excepted? Or how is it again, that the Arabs, the Persians, and all the most refined Eastern nations, have never produced a single painter? Man may be the slave of error, of political circumstance, or of himself; but none but a few hypochondriacs are the slaves of clouds and weather-glasses. The British, it must be confessed, have at present no very great love for the arts; but, nevertheless, they have a much greater than formerly. There was a time when Italy herself wanted taste: it was created by a few great artists, and so it must be in other countries, just as poets and not critics create rules and a taste for poetry. Patronage is generally languid in its birth, and if it does not easily spring up, it must be forced by genius itself. This is the idea a young artist should always have of patronage and of the means of obtaining it. Since WINCKELMANN'S time, his assertion has been disproved, in the best way, by the reputations of REYNOLDS, BARRY, WILSON, and WEST, the Fathers of the English school of painting. These celebrated men have laid a noble foundation, and every thing calls upon their successors to finish the structure — the example already set them, the promise afforded by themselves, the encouraging dawn of public patronage, and the rivalry of the French nation, whom we must endeavour to conquer with mind, now that we see it cannot be done with money.

The Editor has enlarged on these three subjects, because the first is of most immediate importance, and the two others require most immediate care. They will by no means, however, occupy the largest part of the work, the principal feature of which will be *Miscellaneous Literature*, consisting of Essays on Men and Manners, Enquiries into past and present Literature, and all subjects relative to Wit, Morals, and a true Refinement. There will be no direct Review of Books, but new works, as far as they regard the character of the times, will meet with passing notice; and occasional articles will be written to shew the peculiar faults or beauties, injuriousness or utility, of such as have strongly attracted the public attention. In order to obtain proper room for this variety, the REFLECTOR will consist entirely of Original Articles, written purposely for the work, to the exclusion of unnecessary matter, of plagiarisms from Newspapers and Reviews, and of long extracts from books of the day. The Editor will never be tempted to supply the deficiencies of matter, or to serve the purposes of literary quacks, by such letters as, "Sir, permit me to recommend to the notice of your *impartial* and *enlightened* readers," or, — "Mr. Editor, — Sir, allow me through the medium of your *invaluable* Miscellany," &c. &c.

These are the first tricks to be reformed, both on the side of Editor and Correspondent, as tending to degrade the true spirit of literature. Not a page will be wasted on market-prices, or stock-prices, or accounts of the weather, or histories of fashion, or obituaries that give a few weeks' renown for so many shillings. Hides and velvet-collars have, it is true, their rise and fall as well as kingdoms, but then they have distinct interests of their own, and should be left to their respective professors:—the REFLECTOR is determined not to show its ignorance on the subject, and will deviate neither into patterns, nor whip-clubs, nor portraits of "public characters," nor, in short, into any "embellishments" whatever, but such as may be supplied by the wit and knowledge of its Correspondents. The trifles of an age have undoubtedly their connection, sometimes too great a one, with its general character, and they may be handed down as a part of the portrait, just as our ancestors come down to us in their ruffles and periwigs; but the best artists are not those who attend most to these decorations; the true spirit of the likeness is in the man himself — in his air and attitude — and in the mind that looks out of his general aspect. — In a word, it is this *mind*, which the REFLECTOR will endeavour to pourtray; and the Proprietors will spare no industry, the only talent for which they can vouch, to delineate and to call forth the proper expression in those features of the age, which regard its present interests with mankind and its future character with posterity.

THE INDICATOR NO. I

OCTOBER 13, 1819

There is a bird in the interior of Africa, whose habits would rather seem to belong to the interior of Fairy-land: but they have been well authenticated. It indicates to honey-hunters, where the nests of wild bees are to be found. It calls them with a cheerful cry, which they answer; and on finding itself recognized, flies and hovers over a hollow tree containing the honey. While they are occupied in collecting it, the bird goes to a little distance, where he observes all that passes; and the hunters, when they have helped themselves, take care to leave him his portion of the food. — This is the CUCULUS INDICATOR *of Linnæus, otherwise called the Moroc, Bee Cuckoo, or Honey Bird.*

> *There he arriving round about doth flie,*
> *And takes survey with busie, curious eye:*
> *Now this, now that, he tasteth tenderly.*
> — SPENSER

It is the object of this periodical work to notice any subjects whatsoever within the range of the editor's knowledge or reading. He will take them up as they happen to suggest themselves, and endeavour to point out their essence to the reader, so as at once to be brief and satisfactory. The subjects will chiefly consist of curious recollections of biography; short disquisitions on men and things; the most interesting stories in history or fiction told over again, with an eye to their proper appreciation by unvulgar minds; and now and then a few original verses. Indeed, the whole matter, whatever the subject may be, will be strictly original, in one sense of the word; and it will be the editor's aim, as well as a part of his own pleasure, to render it all as entertaining as he can. To the unvulgar he exclusively addresses himself; but he begs it to be particularly understood that in this description of persons are to be included all those who, without having had a classical education, would have turned it to right account; just as all those are to be excluded who, in spite of that "discipline of humanity," think ill of the nature which they degrade, and vulgarly confound the vulgar with the uneducated.

The Indicator will attend to no subject whatsoever of immediate or temporary interest. His business is with honey in the old woods. The editor has enough to agitate his spirits during the present eventful times, in another periodical work; and he is willing to be so agitated: but as he is accustomed to use his pen, as habitually as a bird his pinion, and to betake himself with it into the nests and bowers of more lasting speculations, when he has done with public ones, he is determined to keep these haunts of his recreation free from all noise and wrangling, both for his own pleasure and for those who may chuse to accompany him.

The Indicator will appear every Wednesday morning, at an hour early enough for the breakfast-table; and though the subjects will not be temporary or those of the moment, they will be written as much at the moment as if they were; so that there will still be a certain freshness of intercourse between the editor and his readers.

DIFFICULTY OF FINDING A NAME FOR A WORK OF THIS KIND

Never did gossips, when assembled to determine the name of a new-born child, whose family was full of conflicting interests, experience half the difficulty which an author finds in settling the title for a periodical work. There is generally some paramount uncle, or prodigious third cousin, who is silently understood to have the chief claims, and to the golden lustre of whose face the clouds of hesitation and jealousy gradually give way. But these children of the brain have no godfather at hand: and then their single appellation is bound to comprise as many public interests, as all the Christian names of a French or a German prince. It is to be modest: it is to be expressive: it is to be new: it is to be striking: it is to have something in it equally intelligible to a man of plain understanding, and surprising for the man of imagination: — in one word, it is to be impossible. How far we have succeeded in the attainment of this happy nonentity, we leave others to judge. There is one good thing however which the hunt after a title is sure to realize; — a good deal of despairing mirth. We were visiting a friend the other night, who can do anything for a book but give it a title; and after many grave and ineffectual attempts to furnish one for the present, the company, after the fashion of Rabelais, and with a chair-shaking merriment which he might have joined in himself, fell to turning a hopeless thing into a jest. It was like that exquisite picture of a set of laughers in Shakspeare: —

> One rubbed his elbow, thus; and fleered, and swore
> A better speech was never spoke before:
> Another, with his finger and his thumb,
> Cried "Via! We will do't, come what will come!"
> The third he capered, and cried, "All goes well!"
> The fourth turned on the toe, and down he fell.
> With that they all did tumble on the ground,
> With such a zealous laughter, so profound,
> That in this spleen ridiculous, appears,
> To check their laughter, passion's solemn tears.
>   LOVE'S LABOUR LOST

Some of the names had a meaning in their absurdity, such as the Adviser, or Helps for Composing; — the Cheap Reflector, or Every Man His Own Looking-Glass; – the Retailer, or Every Man His Own Other Man's Wit; – Nonsense, To be Continued. Others were laughable by the mere force of contrast, as the Crocodile, or Pleasing Companion; – Chaos, or the Agreeable Miscellany; – the Fugitive Guide; – the Foot Soldier, or Flowers of Wit; – Bigotry, or the Cheerful Instructor; – the Polite Repository of Abuse; – Blood, being a Collection of Light Essays. Others were sheer ludicrousness and extravagance, as the Pleasing Ancestor; the Silent Remarker; the Tart; the Leg of Beef, by a Layman; the Ingenious Hatband; the Boots of Bliss; the Occasional Diner; the Tooth-ache; Recollections of a Very Unpleasant Nature; Thoughts on Taking up a Pair of Snuffers; Thoughts on a Barouche-Box; Thoughts on a Hill of Considerable Eminence; Mediations on a Pleasing Idea; Materials for Drinking; the Knocker, No. I.; – the Hippopotamus Entered at Stationers' Hall; the Pianoforte of Paulus Æmilius; the Seven Sleepers at Cards; the Arabian Nights on Horseback: – with an infinite number of other mortal murders of common sense, which rose to "push us from our stools," and which none but the wise or good-natured would think of laughing at.

THE INDICATOR NO. II

OCTOBER 20, 1819

One or two persons, we understand, have supposed that the present periodical work will interfere with the literary part of another, in which the Editor has long been concerned. This is a great mistake. *The Examiner* will continue to be more literary, as well as painstaking in every other respect, than it has ever been. It will have more than the usual literature, for instance, connected with politics and criticism, – especially the latter. Indeed, should the new paper injure the old one, it would be dropped. The fact is, that as far as the Editor is concerned, *The Examiner* is to be regarded as the reflection of his public literature, and the *Indicator* of his private. In the one he has a sort of public meeting with his friends: in the other, a more retired one. *The Examiner* is his tavern-room for politics, for political pleasantry, for criticism upon the theatres and living writers. *The Indicator* is his private room, his study, his retreat from public care and criticism, with the reader who chuses to accompany him.

* * * * * * * * *

THE INDICATOR AND COMPANION, 1834. PART I

INTRODUCTION

THE INDICATOR, a series of papers originally published in weekly numbers, having been long out of print, and repeated calls having been made for it among the book-sellers, the author has here made a selection, comprising the greater portion of the articles, and omitting such only as he unwillingly put forth in the hurry of periodical publication, or as seemed otherwise unsuited for present publication, either by the nature of their disquisitions, or from containing commendatory criticisms now rendered superfluous by the reputation of the works criticised.

THE COMPANION, a subsequent publication of the same sort, has been treated in the like manner.

The author has little further to say, by way of advertisement to these volumes except that both the works were written with the same view of inculcating a love of nature and imagination, and of furnishing a sample of the enjoyment which they afford; and he cannot give a better proof of that enjoyment, as far as he was capable of it, than by stating, that both were written during times of great trouble with him, and both helped him to see much of that fair play between his own anxieties and his natural cheerfulness, of which an indestructible belief in the good and the beautiful has rendered him perhaps not undeserving.

London, December 6, 1833

THE LIBERAL. 1822

VERSE AND PROSE FROM THE SOUTH

PREFACE

We are not going to usher in our publication with any pomp
of prospectus. We mean to be very pleasant and ingenious, of
course; but decline proving it beforehand by a long common-
place. The greater the flourish of trumpets nowadays, the
more suspicious what follows. Whatever it may be our luck
to turn out, we at least wave our privilege of having the way
prepared for us by our own mouth-pieces, – by words with
long tails, and antitheses two and two. If we succeed, so much
the better. If not, we shall at all events not die of the previous question, like an honest proposal in Parliament.

But we are forced to be prefatory, whether we would or
no: for others, it seems, have been so anxious to furnish us
with something of this sort, that they have blown the trumpet
for us; and done us the honour of announcing, that nothing
less is to ensue, than a dilapidation of all the outworks of civ-
ilized society. Such at least, they say, is our intention; and
such would be the consequences, if they, the trumpeters, did
not take care by counter-blasts, to puff the said outworks up
again. We should be more sensible of this honour if it did not
arise from a confusion of ideas. They say that we are to cut
up religion, morals, and everything that is legitimate; – a
pretty carving. It only shows what they really think of their
own opinions on those subjects. The other day a ministerial
paper said, that "robes and coronations were the strongholds
of royalty." We do not deny it; but if such is their strength,
what is their weakness? If by religion they meant anything

really worthy of divine or human beings; if by morals, they meant the only true morals, justice and beneficence; if by everything legitimate, they meant but half of what their own laws and constitutions have provided against the impudent pretensions of the despotic, – then we should do our best to leave religion and morals as we found them, and show their political good faith at least half as much respect as we do. But when we know, – and know too from our intimacy with various classes of people, – that there is not a greater set of hypocrites in the world than these pretended teachers of the honest and inexperienced part of our countrymen; – when we know that their religion, even when it is in earnest on any point (which is very seldom), means the most ridiculous and untenable notions of the DIVINE BEING, and in all other cases means nothing but the Bench of Bishops; – when we know that their morals consist for the most part in a secret and practical contempt of their own professions, and for the least and best part, of a few dull examples of something a little more honest, clapped in front to make a show and a screen, and weak enough to be made tools against all mankind; – and when we know, to crown all, that their "legitimacy," as they call it, is the most unlawful of all lawless and impudent things, tending, under pretence that the whole world are as corrupt and ignorant as themselves, to put it at the mercy of the most brute understandings among them, – men by their very education in these pretensions, rendered the least fit to sympathise with their fellow-men, and as unhappy, after all, as the lowest of their slaves; – when we know all this, and see nine-tenths of all the intelligent men in the world alive to it, and as resolved as we are to oppose it, then indeed we are willing to accept the title of enemies to religion, morals, and legitimacy, and hope to do our duty with all becoming profaneness accordingly. God defend us from the piety of thinking him a monster! God defend us from the morality of slaves and turn-coats, and from the legitimacy of half a dozen lawless old gentlemen, to whom, it seems, human nature is an estate in fee.

The object of our work is not political, except inasmuch as all writing now-a-days must involve something to that effect, the connection between politics and all other subjects of interest to mankind having been discovered, never again to be done away. We wish to do our work quietly, if people will let us, – to contribute our liberalities in the shape of Poetry, Essays, Tales, Translations, and other amenities, of which kings themselves may read and profit, if they are not afraid of seeing their own faces in every species of inkstand. Italian Literature in particular will be a favourite subject with us; and so was German and Spanish to have been, till we lost the accomplished Scholar and Friend who was to share our task; but perhaps we may be able to get a supply of the scholarship, though not of the friendship. It may be our good fortune to have more than one foreign correspondent, who will be an acquisition to the reader. In the meantime we must do our best by ourselves; and the reader may be assured he shall have all that is in us, clear and candid at all events, if nothing else; for

> We love to pour out all ourselves as plain
> As downright SHIPPEN or as old MONTAIGNE

There are other things in the world besides kings, or even sycophants. There is one thing in particular with which we must help to bring the polite world acquainted, which is NATURE. Life really does not consist, entirely, of clubs and ballrooms, of a collar made by Wilkins, and of the west end of the town. We confess we have a regard for the Dandies, properly so called; not the spurious race who take their title from their stays; we mean the pleasant and pithy personages who began the system, and who had ideas as well as bibs in their head. But it was on that account. We like them, because they partook of the ETHERIDGES and SUCKLINGS of old: and why were the ETHERIDGES and SUCKLINGS better than their neighbours, but because they inherited from Old Mother Wit as well as Mother West-end, and partook of the prerogatives of Nature? We have a regard for certain modern Barons, as well as those who got the Great Charter for us; but is it for those who would keep or for those who would give up the Charter? Is it for those who identify themselves with every feeble King John, or for those who have some of "GOD ALMIGHTY's Nobility" in them as well as their own? Assuredly for the latter, — assuredly for those who have something in them "which surpasses show," and which the breath of a puffing and blowing legitimate cannot unmake.

Be present then, and put life into our work, ye Spirits, not of the GAVESTONES and the DESPENSERS, but of the JOHN O'GAUNTS, the WICKLIFFES, and the CHAUCERS; — be present, not the slaves and sycophants of King HENRY the Eighth — (whose names we have forgotten) but the HENRY HOWARDS, the SURREYS, and the WYATTS; — be present, not ye other rapscallions and "booing" slaves of the court of King JAMIE, but ye BUCHANANS and ye WALTER RALEIGHS; — be present, not ye bed-chamber lords, flogging-boys, and mere soldiers, whosoever ye are, from my Lord THINGUMEE in King CHARLES's time, down to the immortal Duke of WHAT's-HIS-NAME now flourishing; but the HERBERTS, the HUTCHINSONS, the LOCKES, the POPES, and the PETERBOROUGHS; — be present, not ye miserable tyrants, slaves, bigots, or turncoats of any party, not ye LAUDS or ye LAUDERDALES, ye Legitimate Pretenders (for so ye must now be called), ye TITUS OATESES, BEDLOWS, GARDINERS, SACHEVERELLS, and SOUTHEYS; but ye MILTONS and ye MARVELLS, ye HOADLEYS, ADDISONS, and STEELES, ye SOMERSES, DORSETS, and PRIORS, and all who have thrown light and life upon man, instead of darkness and death; who have made him a thing of hope and freedom, instead of despair and slavery; a being progressive, instead of a creeping creature retrograde; – if we have no pretensions to your genius, we at least claim the merit of loving and admiring it, and of longing to further its example.

We wish the title of our work to be taken in its largest acceptation, old as well as new, – but always in the same spirit of admiring and assisting, rather than of professing. We just as much disclaim any assumption in it before the wise, as we disclaim any false modesty before all classes. All that we mean is, that we are advocates of every species of liberal knowledge, and that, by natural consequence in these times, we go the full length in matters of opinions with large bodies of men who are called LIBERALS. At the same time, when we say the full length, we mean something very different from what certain pretended Liberals, and all the Illiberals, will take it to be; for it is by the very reason of going to that length, in its most liberal extreme – "Ay, ay," interrupts some old clubhouse Gentleman, in a buff waistcoat and red-face, – "Now you talk sense. Extremes meet. *Verbum sap.* I am a Liberal myself, if you come to that, and devilish liberal I am. I gave for instance five guineas out of the receipts of my sinecure to the Irish sufferers; but that is between ourselves. You mean, that there are good hearty fellows in all parties, and that the great business is to balance them properly; – to let the people talk, provided they do no harm, and to let Governments go on as they do, have done, and will do for ever. Good, – good. I'll take in your journal myself; – here's to the success of it; – only don't make it too violent, you rogues; – don't spoil the balance. (God! I've spilt my bumper!) Cut up SOUTHEY as much as you please. We all think him as great a coxcomb as you do, and he bores us to death; but spare the King and the Ministers and all that, particularly Lord CASTLEREAGH and the Duke of WELLINGTON. D——d gentlemanly fellow, CASTLEREAGH, as you know; and besides he's dead. Shocking thing – shocking. It was all nonsense about his being so cold-hearted, and doing Ireland so much harm. He was the most gentlemanly of men. Wars must be carried on; Malthus has proved that millions must be slaughtered from time to time. The nonsense about that is as stupid as the cry about the game-laws and those infernal villains the poachers, who ought all to be strung up like hares: and as to Ireland, it is flying in the face of Providence to think that such horrible things could happen there, and be prevented by *earthly* means, – *earthly* means, sir. Lord CASTLEREAGH himself referred us to Providence in all these unavoidable matters, and he was right; – but to think of his cutting his own throat – Good God! so very gentlemanly a man, and in the height of his power! It is truly shocking! As to WELLINGTON, he's not so gentlemanly a man, certainly; but then neither is CANNING, if you come to that. He cannot make speeches, I own; but no more can the king or my lord MARYBOROUGH, or a hundred other eminent characters, and he does not make such cursed awkward blunders as poor CASTLEREAGH used to do. He has not got a very wise look, they say; but – I don't know, – it's soldierlike, I think; and if you come to that, what a strange fellow old BLUCHER looked, and SUWARROW, and all those; and between ourselves, the reigning Monarchs are a set of as common-looking gentry, as you'd wish to see in a summer's day; so I don't know what people would have. No – no – you really mustn't speak against WELLINGTON. Besides, he prosecutes."

We beg the reader's pardon in behalf of our worthy interrupter. Whatever may be his right estimation of his friends, we need not say that he misinterprets our notions of liberality,

which certainly do not consist either in making the sort of confusion, or keeping the sort of peace, which he speaks of. There
are, if he pleases, very silly fellows to be found in most parties,
and these may be good enough to be made tools of by the
clever ones; but to confound all parties themselves with one
another, which is the real end of these pretended liberalities,
and assume that none of them are a jot better or worse than
the other, and may contain just as good and generous people, —
this is to confound liberality with illiberality, narrow views
with large, the instincts of a selfish choice with those of a generous one, and in the best and most imposing instances, the
mere amenities and ordinary virtues of private life (which
may be only a graceful selfishness, unless they go farther)
with the noblest and boldest sympathies in behalf of the human race. It is too late in the day to be taken in with this kind
of cant; even by the jolliest of placemen in all the benevolence of his bumpers. The Duke of WELLINGTON is a great
officer, "after his kind." We do not mean at court, where he
is a very little officer, and condescends to change his Mar-
shal's staff for the stick of a Lord in Waiting. But he is a
good hunting captain, — a sort of human setter. We allow
him all his praise in that respect, and only wish he had not
confounded the rights of nations with those of a manor. What
does he mean too by treating public meetings with contempt?
And above all, what did he mean by that extremely odd assumption of the didactic, about teaching a "great moral les-
son!" As to Lord CASTLEREAGH, he was one of the most il-
liberal and vindictive of statesmen, if we must use that word
for every petty retainer, whom a bad system swells for a time
into a part of its own unnatural greatness. Look at his famous
Six Acts! Look at his treatment of BONAPARTE, his patronage of such infamous journals as the *Beacon*, his fondness for
imprisoning, and for what his weak obstinacy calls his other
strong measures. But he is dead, and people are now called

upon to be liberal! Let us be so, in God's name, in the general
sense we have of the infirmities of human nature; but it is
one thing to be liberal in behalf of the many, and another
thing to be exclusively so in behalf of the few. Have the consequences of Lord CASTLEREAGH'S actions died with him?
Are the Six Acts dead? Are thousands of the Irish *living*?
We will give a specimen of the liberality of these new de-
manders of liberality. The other day, when one of the noblest
of human beings, PERCY SHELLEY, who had more religion in
his very differences with religion, than thousands of your
church-and-state men, was lost on the coast of Italy, the
Courier said, that "Mr. PERCY SHELLEY, *a writer of infidel
poetry*, was drowned." Where was the liberality of this cant-
ing insinuation? Where was the decency, or, as it turned out,
the common sense of it? Mr. SHELLEY's death by the waves
was followed by Lord CASTLEREAGH's by his own hand; and
then the cry is for liberal constructions! How could we not
turn such a death against the enemies of Mr. SHELLEY, if we
could condescend to affect a moment's agreement with their
hypocrisy? But the least we can do is to let these people
see, that we know them, and to warn them how they assail
us. The force of our answers will always be proportioned to
the want of liberality in the assailant. This is a liberality, at
all events, upon which our readers may reckon. The rest,
which we were going to say, is this; – that although we condemn by wholesale certain existing demands upon our sub-
mission and credulity, we are not going to discover every
imaginative thing even in a religion to be nonsense, like a
semi-liberalized Frenchman; nor, on the other hand, to denounce all levity and wit to be nonsense and want of feeling,
like a semi-liberalized German. If we are great admirers of
VOLTAIRE, we are great admirers also of GOETHE and SCHIL-
LER. If we pay our homage to DANTE and MILTON, we have

tribute also for the brilliant sovereignties of ARIOSTO and BOCCACCIO.

Wherever, in short, we see the mind of man exhibiting powers of its own, and at the same time helping to carry on the best intentions of human nature, – however it may overdo the matter a little on this side or on that, or otherwise partake of the common frailty through which it passes, – there we recognize the demi-gods of liberal worship; – there we bow down, and own our lords and masters; – there we hope for the final passing away of all obscene worships, however formalized, – of all monstrous sacrifices of the many to the few, however "legitimatized" and besotted.

THE DOGS

TO THE ABUSERS OF THE LIBERAL

[*The Liberal*, vol. i, p. 245]

"GENTLEMEN,"

This little poem is dedicated to you. It is not the wish of *The Liberal* to write satire and personal politics; but if you insist upon our earning a right to be heard with the sword, it must be so. Some persons, it seems, must either do this, or consent to be trampled into silence, let them be as forbearing as they may. That we can forbear, we know well, and so do you: – that we can make you cry out again with non-forbearance, we know also: – but we fight, like the Greeks and Spaniards, to obtain the right and the tranquillity of speech, and not to trample on every body in turn. The satire in the first number of *The Liberal* was produced by those who attacked us before-hand: – the satire in the second is the result of the attacks on the first. It will be for yourselves to judge how soon we are to leave off this boy's-play and cutting of

knuckles. The moment we can turn our swords into plough-
shares and our spears into pruning-hooks, we shall be happy
to cultivate those calmer fields of knowledge, which (with
your leave be it spoken) you are a set of prodigious fools for
not knowing how to look to at once.

ADVERTISEMENT

TO THE SECOND VOLUME OF *THE LIBERAL*

1823

Never was a greater outcry raised among the hypocrites of all
classes, than against this publication. What with the "great
vulgar" protesting, the "small" abusing, lawyers denounc-
ing, "divines" cursing, scandal-mongers bawling, dunces of
all sorts shrieking – all the sore places of the community seem
to have been touched, and the "body politic" agitated accordingly.

> As when the long ear'd, milky mothers wait
> At some sick miser's triple-bolted gate,
> For their defrauded, absent foals they make
> A moan so loud, that all the Guild awake;
> Sore sighs Sir Gilbert, starting at the bray,
> From dreams of millions, and three groats to pay:
> So swells each windpipe: ass intones to ass,
> Harmonic twang! of leather, horn, and brass;
> Such as from lab-ring lungs th' enthusiast blows,
> High sounds, attempered to the vocal nose;
> Or such as bellow from the deep divine:
> There, Webster! peal'd thy voice; and, Whitfield! thine;
> But far o'er all sonorous Blackmore's strain:
> Walls, steeples, skies, bray back to him again.
> In Tottenham fields the brethren with amaze,
> Prick all their ears up, and forget to graze!

Long Chancery Lane, retentive, rolls the sound,
And courts to courts return it round and round.
DUNCIAD

All these people deserve no better answer than a laughing quotation. But we will just admonish some well-meaning persons, not over strong in their understandings, that with respect to the religious part of the business, they are most grossly and "irreligiously" taken in, if they suffer themselves to be persuaded, that it is we who would lessen the divinity of what is really divine. It is these pretended "divines" and their abettors, who lessen it;—those raisers-up of absurd and inhuman imaginations, which they first impudently confound with divine things, and then, because we shew the nonsense of the imaginations, as impudently call their exposers blasphemers. Were we inclined to retort their own terms upon them, we should say that there was nothing in the world more "blasphemous" than such charges of blasphemy. The whole secret is just what we have stated. They first assume unworthy notions of the Divine Spirit, and then because that very Spirit is in fact vindicated from their degradations by an exposure of the absurdity and impossibility of such notions, they assume a divine right to denounce the vindicators, and to rouse up all the fears, weakness, and ignorance of society, in defence of the degredation. Of this stuff have the "Scribes, Pharisees, and Hypocrites" in all ages been made, whenever established opinion was to be divested of any of its corruptions. "He blasphemeth!" quoth the modern tribunal. "Great is Diana of the Ephesians!" quoth the *Quarterly*. *This* is the point, which persons who undertake to be didactic in Reviews, should answer; and not a hundred things which we never said.

There is a more generous indignation which we allow might be felt by some persons upon another point, but still owing to real want of information on the subject. We allude to what has been said in *The Liberal* of the late King. The *Vision of Judgment* was written in a fit of indignation and disgust at Mr. Southey's nonsense; and we confess that had we seen a copy of it in Italy, before it went to press (for we had none by us) we should have taken more pains to explain one or two expressions with regard to that Prince. Had the Preface also, entrusted to Mr. Murray, been sent, as it ought to have been, to the new publisher, much of the unintended part of the effect produced upon weak minds would have been explained away at once; — that effect, which the hypocritical enemies of *The Liberal* at once delighted to assist in producing, and most pretended to deprecate. But the virtues of the late King, though of a negative kind, were of a kind nevertheless exceedingly calculated to excite a great many feelings in favour of him in a society like that of England; while his vices (pardon us, dear self-love of our countrymen, for supposing that you *have* vices) were equally calculated to be overlooked in a certain general blindness prevailing on that subject. Yet to those vices, — extreme self-will for instance, sullenness of purpose, a strong natural vindictiveness, &c. was owing the bloody protraction of the American War: to those vices, as well as to Mr. Pitt's haughty sympathy with them, was mainly owing the general war against liberty which was roused among the despots of the continent: and if certain staid and well-intentioned people suppose, that persons quite as moral and pious as themselves, could not hold the late King in a light very different from their own, and much more revolting than even we hold it, they are most egregiously mistaken. What was thought of George the Third's natural character by a man of the highest respectability, who knew him intimately at court, — to wit, his own Governor when Prince of Wales, — may be seen by those *who wish to do us justice*, in the Memoirs of James, Earl of Waldegrave, published by the aforesaid Mr. Murray. See also Dr. Franklin's Life, Junius, and the opinion of Mr. Southey's friend, the author of Gebir. What the Earl of Waldegrave prophecied of that character, may be seen also in Mr. Murray's publication. We think that prophecy came to pass. The most pious and virtuous person we ever knew, even in the ordinary sense of those terms (and she might have stood by the side of the most virtuous, in the most extraordinary) thought so too, and taught some of us to think so in our childhood. The ruin of her family and prospects was brought upon her, to her knowledge, by that Prince's temper and obstinacy, and though the strict religious way in which she was brought up might have induced her to carry too far her opinion of the *cause* of that calamitous and awful affliction under which he suffered, the parasites of his memory are under a much greater mistake, when instead of turning their knowledge on that point to its great and proper account (which has never yet been hinted even in this great nation of reasoning freemen!) they fancy they can put down all thoughts upon such subjects, and all the unfortunate consequences of such *facts*, by raising a hypocritical cry against a few hasty expressions, uttered in that very spirit of sympathy with the community at large, which they count as nothing.

We cannot close this Advertisement without adding our cordial voice (truly humble on the present occasion) to the universal harmony prevailing in England on the subject of the glorious rights and equally glorious behavior of Spain. We must also say, how much surprise and relief have been afforded to us by the political plain-speaking (granting even it ends in little more) of the accomplished person who has succeeded that vizor of a statesman, Lord Castlereagh.

THE CHAT OF THE WEEK

A COMPENDIUM OF ALL TOPICS OF PUBLIC INTEREST, ORIGINAL AND SELECT

JUNE 5, 1830

PROSPECTUS

The publication, here announced, has been suggested by the popularity of those departments in the Newspapers which are devoted to miscellaneous intelligence, and which generally consist of paragraphs equally short and amusing. Many a reader, who cares little for politics, is willing to have as much as an Editor can give him of entertaining paragraph; and those who care for any subject in particular, or for all subjects, would willingly have them divested of what is stale and unprofitable, just as they like to have their lettuces served up without the outer leaves. Now it will be our business to get rid of the outer leaves of everything, and to serve up the heart and soul of it.

It is not our intention to be always as short as the *chat* or *multum in parvo* of a newspaper; but as our object is to omit nothing that is of interest, and to retain nothing that is dull, our paragraphs, for the most part, will be shorter than otherwise.[1] We have no limits as to subjects. We shall take the whole round of observation – the State, the Drama, the New Publications, New Music, Manners and Customs, the Town, the Country, the "Great World" (meaning a place about three miles long), and the Little World (that is to say, all

---

[1] The reader will smile to see how little we have kept our word on this point; but we trust he will not be dissatisfied. The truth is, we were not prepared to meet with so many articles, at once so long and so interesting.

the rest of the Globe). If the word *Chat* be thought too humble for some of our pages, it will be an objection we shall be very glad to hear of. Nevertheless there are few things in this world better than real good chat; plainly so called. We shall be happy, if what we write ourselves shall be thought to belong to it. Higher honours will be willingly conceded to those from whom we extract.

The plan of our pamphlet is this. There will be an *Original Article* at the head of it, *on the principal subject of interest that has occurred during the week*. This will be followed by a compilation of the best passages in the newspapers, relating to *Politics*, the *Houses of Parliament, etc.*: not whole articles (unless the matter is of great interest throughout), but the best passages out of articles, as well as any separate paragraphs that may strike us. If we meet with an article, for instance, which contains but one striking passage, or which, however good throughout, contains but one passage that is suitable to our purpose, *that* passage only we select. It will be the same with regard to *Theatricals*, which come next in order — to the *Fine Arts* — to *New Books*, and so on, concluding with the *Miscellaneous* Department, which will be most abundant of any. To such of the paragraphs as suggest remarks of our own, we shall append them by way of comment; so that the publication may be described, in general, as a compendium of all topics of public interest, with an original article at the head of it, and *occasional notes throughout*, the whole putting the reader in possession, at the least expense, and in the most entertaining manner, of the *Facts, Opinions*, and *Clever Sayings* of the week.

When we say that we shall retain nothing that is dull, it is not true in the absolute sense of the word; for we shall sometimes quote a foolish author. But as extremes meet, and as we shall quote no dulness but such as is very exquisite, and nonsense that it would be difficult to match, the effect will be as good as wit. Besides, justice will thus be done to all parties. Nothing will be omitted that is convertible to the reader's pleasure; he will see what we can go through for his sake; and the man who was as dull as a Directory in his own pages, will find himself entertaining in ours.

We think it proper to declare, at the same time, that we shall not force this involuntary agreeableness upon anybody who does not take upon himself to dictate to the public in bad taste, or with an unworthy spirit. Neither shall we be tempted to expose anyone, dull or otherwise, who speaks in his own name, and is not to be ranked among that numerous and unprincipled class of persons who infect the high roads of Literature of the present day, and have been well characterized as "fellows with crape over their faces." If it fall in our way to notice any of these persons, and we know their names, by name they will be noticed. Our own names will always be forthcoming to such as have a right to demand them; and, behaving like honest men ourselves, we shall respect the claims of none but the honest. Candour and merit will never be without our good word; neither will an honourable enemy be confounded with a dishonourable. We desire no favour ourselves, if we do not show ourselves capable of doing justice to the merits of all parties, enemies as well as friends.

And now, gentle reader, if thou dost not like this very candid, intelligent, and courteous statement (all epithets belonging, time immemorial to thyself), if thou dost not take our New Publication with thy tea, or thy dessert, or thy cigar, or thy next good resolution, or with the paper which thou takest already (provided thou art rich enough to have two), "Why," as Falstaff says, "thou art not the man we took thee for." Certainly thou art not like one of us: for we plainly confess our attachment to the good things of other people, and should have liked nothing better than a work of the same sort from other hands, if we had not taken it upon our own.

THE TATLER

A Daily Paper of Literature, Fine Arts, Music, and the Stage

SEPTEMBER 4, 1830

TO THE READERS OF THE CHAT OF THE WEEK

This opening article began with some record of difficulties with the "Stamp office" about the legality of a new shape given to the Chat of the Week. To avoid dispute Leigh Hunt started this altogether new journal.– Ed.

We have taken an illustrious title for our new paper; but we are not vain enough to be modest on that score, or deprecate comparison with the original possessor. There is nothing in the humbler nature of our work to provoke it. We borrow the title simply because the journal, called the Spectator, has led the way to this adoption of a popular name; and because in availing ourselves of the example, and being of ripe years enough to choose a clan and a god-father, we prefer the one whose name we are fondest of. If we are not ill-natured, not insincere, and not without an eye to the common good in what may seem to be the most personal of our hostilities, the original would not be ashamed of us.

Our first number is a specimen of what The Tatler is generally intended to be. It will consist of entertaining extracts from books with occasional criticism; of theatrical criticism, written with a love of the subject, and an impartiality, for which we shall claim credit at once, from a reputation for honesty in those matters; of a miscellaneous department for stray passages of any kind; and of any light original articles that may suggest themselves, in prose or verse, and which may be thought suitable to a breakfast-table. The paper will be published the first thing in the morning, with the newspapers of the day, to which we venture to hope it may not be found an unsuitable companion. Orders should be given for it to the regular newsmen. The town will thus have, for the first time these many years, a regular daily paper devoted to literature and criticism; and readers will be reminded of old times and names by the aspect of it. *Poins* had one thing in common with the Prince of Wales: "their legs were both of a thickness." The reader who takes up this paper, and is interested in the title of it, must be informed, that its size and general aspect is that of the original TATLER published in 1709; such as Pope and Addison held in their hands, and that Belinda bent over while the Sylphs were fanning her coffee.

THE TATLER

AUGUST 20, 1831

OUR CHANGE OF PRICE

A member of the Society of Friends, who called the other day at the office of this paper, expressed his regret, that in writing of the change of price, we had not eulogised those who should hereafter take it in, instead of reprobating such as should remain insensible to the claims of our Penny. We acknowledge that this would have been a more Christian proceeding, and that the suggestion is worthy of the mild and by no means unsuccessful community from which it emanates. But we beg him to consider the provocation. We know what we have in store for the buyer of *The Tatler*, how much enjoyment, how much novelty, how many slices of relishing criticism for breakfast, what accounts of new books and old pictures, of music, of exhibitions, of theatres, of thousands of matters going forward, and thousands gone by, and when we consider that any man (if such a man there be) can be aware of all of this, and yet withhold his four farthings, — can say, Knowledge is good, Instruction and Amusement are good, Jones's book is good, Nature, Truth, Love, Wit, Humanity, Merriment and Madame Pasta are good, *but a penny is better*, — we beg leave to know what we are to think of him, or how he is to be sufficiently warned against his error. Let us consider what he does not care for.

He does not care for books.

He does not care for pictures.

He does not care for theatres.

He does not care for exhibitions.

He does not care for the whale.

He does not care for Master Regondi.

He does not care for advertisements.

He does not care for jokes.

He does not care for the most pathetic stories.

He does not care for Shakespeare.

He does not care for Raphael or Titian.

He does not care for Mozart.

He does not care for his boots.

He does not care for a good hat.

He does not care for the Press.

He does not care for Reform, and consequently not for the King.

He does not care for Miss Inverarity.

He does not care for any body.

He does not care for his wife (or he would take the Tatler on purpose for her).

He does not care for his breakfast (except grossly).

He does not care for his reputation.

He does not care what the servants think of him.

He does not care for Paganini.

He does not care for the Irish.

He does not care for the French.

He does not care for the Poles.

He does not care for posterity.

He does not care for Chaucer.

He has no care, prospective or retrospective.

He does not care for his face (the expression of which is modified).

He does not care to begin his day in a good temper.

He does not care for the opinion of all the readers of the Tatler.

He does not care for his pounds and eleven pences (and being penny-wise he is all the rest foolish).

He does not care for a cigar, nor a cup of coffee, nor his bottle, nor his chat, nor his friends, nor his muffin (for how can he truly relish any of these things, if his taste be always infected with the copper twange of his penny?).

Therefore he will soon not be able to have a muffin: for a muffin costs a penny, and with what face can he buy a muffin, and refuse to buy a Tatler?

Hence, having no muffin, and beginning for want of ideas, to think that he wants nothing hot or comfortable, he will soon have no fire in his room, nay, not in the kitchen; thus realising the melancholy description of the poet, —

> A penny saved is a penny got:
> Firm to this scoundrel maxim keepeth he,
> Till it hath quench'd his fire, and banished his pot.

The inevitable conclusion is that his servants and friends will all leave him: the dog whom he quartered in the butcher's next door, will leave him: even the old woman who nursed his father, will not stay: he will die of inanition, in a cold room, on a bed that has not been made for the last six months, holding a prospectus of the *Tatler* in one hand, and a penny in the other, and the Coroner's inquest, after refusing to sit on him, (on account of the horrible sharpness of his bones) will bring in a verdict of "Died for want of reading the penny journal."

We say without hesitation the penny journal, for though there are minds of an aspiring order, who think there is no dignity in a charge under eight farthings, and are in alarm for the respectability of a paper which costs but four, we own we cannot attain to the height of their conclusions, especially when we reflect that the greatest fortunes are made up of pence, – that if our journal were published quarterly and charged so many shillings, the sum would only amount to so many fractions a day, – and finally, that the loftiest people in the land consent to help themselves out of these our very pence, and to have their names in the pension-list as receiving so many thousands of pounds, nineteen shillings, fourpence half-penny!

Having thus disposed of the unhappy individual who declines taking us in, let us see what sort of taste is exhibited, and what pleasures must be enjoyed by him who shall do the reverse, – who shall add himself to our list of subscribers. Imprimis, he cares for everything which the other does *not* care for.

He is a good fellow.

He takes an interest in all that concerns humanity.

He loves all that is loveable.

He hates tyranny, hypocrisy, bigotry, cruelty, stinginess, absentees, a bad breakfast, and the boroughmongers.

He does not despise a penny, but he is not a slave to it.

His friends like him.

He can be serious, and yet can laugh heartily.

He says to a man fresh from the country, "Good God! what, don't you take in the Tatler?"

He makes a point of getting us two subscribers. (This is one of his most engaging qualities.)

When he eats a bun, he says, "Who would think that a *Tatler* does [1] no more?"

He thinks, with the greatest genius of the age, it is wise to begin the day with a few pleasant thoughts; (such, for example, as are to be found in this paper).

He is of opinion, that the idle man is the less uncomfortable for such a beginning; that women look handsomer for it; that the uneasy are encouraged by it; the gay get reflection by it; and the man of business goes to his duties the more cheerfully for it.

He shows this passage to every one he meets.

He puts a *Tatler* now and then in his pocket.

He thinks there are but two things that warrant a man's being out of temper, — a defeat of liberty, or the paper's not being ready for him at breakfast.

He highly approves of all we have said in this article.

THE TATLER

AUGUST 22, 1831

OUR SUCCESS

There was a ludicrous mistake of the press in our last number. Our reader was described as saying when he eat a bun "Who would think that the *Tatler does* no more?" Now we acknowledge our respect for a bun, and do often eat the same. (They make excellent plum buns for a penny, at Dill's, the corner of Poland St., Oxford Street.) But however temper-

---

[1] See next article.

ate our food, we cannot subsist upon profits of a single number of our journal. The sentence ought to have been, "Who would think that a *Tatler costs* no more? *That* ground of amazement, however surprising is within the known regions of the possible.

Our subscribers will be glad to hear (and our reputation for veracity enables us to feel all the pleasure of saying it) that the sale of our first Penny Number on Saturday, far surpassed our expectations. The sale is going on while we are writing this paragraph. The office on Saturday had a constant succession of visitors, numbers of whom expressed themselves so cordially towards our little journal that we may venture to call them friends. And we have friends of all classes — not "high" and "low" (which is a distinction never to be found in our pages), but rich and poor, the titled and the mechanic, the clever educated, and the clever uneducated, for we hold it impossible that a reader of the *Tatler* should not be clever. The most unlearned knows what he wants, and that is the first step to wisdom. You might as well talk of undiscerning discernment, as of a fool who takes in *The Tatler*.

We are particularly pleased with two circumstances that have come to our knowledge on this occasion; one is that the men of leisure highly approve the attention we mean to pay to "Public amusements," and are bent upon not disposing of themselves between three and four o'clock, till they see what elephant or other amenity we point out to their notice: — the second: that numbers of intelligent men, in the humblest walks of life, have expressed a delight at finding a literary journal cheap enough for them to read, and that too a daily one; so that they can have a paper at breakfast like their richer neighbours, and know about all the amusement and instruction that is going forward. It shall go hard if we do not satisfy them; for we mean to be very industrious; and we can safely declare, that desirous as we are of reaping profits not to be despised by any man, and very welcome to old soldiers of reform, a great part of the *pleasure* with which we labour will arise from the consciousness of contributing food to the present hunger for knowledge. The reader remembers those accomplished biscuits, and that gingerbread of a literary turn, which in his younger days used to convey knowledge as well as food, and even assist the diffusion of some maxim in politics. We intend that our *Tatler* shall be to men, what these were to children. We look upon ourselves as mental confectioners, who turn out, every day, so many batches of a new kind of tart, small and relishing, with a world of inscriptions upon it. And our hand shall be known in the making, as much as Bedreddin's was in that wonderful tart of which we read in the Arabian "Nights" – "Ah!" said his mother, *fainting* (for she had been looking for him all over the world, and suddenly discovered him by this means) "no one but my dear son Bedreddin could have made such a tart!" Now the reader shall not faint, for we do not mean him to lose us; but he shall say, as he devours our paragraphs, "This is my *Tatler's* cookery all over."

In short, our readers are responsible for the competent way in which we talk, for they have made us very happy by their Saturday's treatment of us, and animal spirits are sooner raised in us than put down.

We present to them all a hearty and zealous ☞

THE TATLER

AUGUST 23, 1831

OF THOSE WHO OUGHT TO READ US

Having given a general character of the individuals who shall or shall not take in this paper, we proceed to show how incumbent it is upon all *classes* of people to read us. And first of those who go first on all occasions, or ought to do so, – the women.

Women are especially bound to patronise us, from the great love we bear them; and from the zeal we manifest in advancing their social condition. We praise and patronise *them* always. We exhort them to be as charming as God made them; to be sincere, merry, and open-hearted. And we shew them the way. We are always blowing trumpets for them, and clearing the road for their progress; nay, we have put them first in our playbills, an example that has been followed, to its immortal honour, by the theatre at that old court-end of the town, Sadler's Wells, – the neighbourhood of Queen Elizabeth and her gallant knights. You may know a reader of *The Tatler* at the theatre, by the pains he takes to get a woman a seat, or his giving up his own to her, if there is no other. If you see a woman reading a paper of a small folio size, and looking particularly charming, over it, it is a *Tatler*. It has the art of fetching out all that is good and beautiful in her face.

Statesmen must read our paper, in order that they may know what is thought in certain speculative quarters of the community, very influential on the next generation. If they leave us out, they are likely to make horrid mistakes in that direction.

Reformers must read us out of our love to reform; and *anti-reformers,* to know what they have to answer; otherwise, by this time next year, they will find themselves talking in a huge desert – all the rest of the world having moved forward, and left them alone.

Rich men must be acquainted with us, that they may know all about exhibitions, theatres, new books, etc., and what an excessive enjoyment there is in the proper use of a penny: and the *Poor* must read us that they may see how much utility a penny can bring them, and what numberless things we say for their benefit to the Rich. The rich man, who does not take in our paper, will have servants in his house, who should know more about operas, poems, pictures, etc., than he; which would be very monstrous. His kitchen shall be full of Dodsleys, and he not know how critical they are on his ignorance; – what things they are looking at him at table, while he is talking over his soup, and showing his want of Tatlerism. Furthermore, we must tell the most accomplished of this class, that *their newspaper is incomplete without us.* The Tatler is a companion to the newspaper, and furnishes every day what is not to be expected in the other journals. A play, a new book, or an exhibition is criticised occasionally in the newspapers, but the notice of these things is our business. They are our news. While the newspaper man is going to the House of Lords or Commons, we are setting out for Drury Lane or the Haymarket; and while he is asleep in the morning, in consequence of Sir James's speeches, we are up, and seeing the whale's skeleton or the British Gallery. What is the rich man to do with his time if he does not know what there is to be seen? or how is he to bear his existence, without knowing whether the new phenomenon has answered? For the newspapers may advertise things; it is we who criticise them; and a man is not to venture lightly into a whale's mouth. He should know what he is to expect.

The liberal professions must all read us. We are no takers of physic, nor talkers about it. When people talk to us about physic, we long to chuck mud in their faces. We agree with Dryden: –

> Better to hunt in fields for health unbought,
> Than fee the doctor for a nauseous draught,
> The wise for cure on exercise depend.

But the *surgeon* has much of our respect; and the true physician (who is not a mere giver of physic, but a humanist *par excellence*, and a liberal enquirer into "all the ills that flesh is heir to") has never found greater eulogy than from our pen. Our love of the Cullens, and Garths, and Sydenhams, is notorious. Besides, it is part of the physician's business to know and recommend whatsoever is good for the spirits of his patients; and a Tatler is physic for the soul. Taken with breakfast, it improves the flavour of the tea, and wonderfully helps digestion. It is a kind of *Sage* between the bread and butter, much better for the purpose than the leaves of the plant so-called. If there is no sunshine in the room, it supplies it. Also, ham and eggs. And there is no oppression afterwards. If a man has never so fine a breakfast, and no Tatler to it, the pretensions of his table are inferior to those of the simplest. The best and healthiest of his refinements is absent. We defy him to eat ever so much, and yet feel as light and comfortable after it, as he who has taken nothing but tea, bread and butter, and Tatler. Let the physician, therefore, see that he prescribes it. There is only one disadvantage in it (if disadvantage it can be called), and that is, that if once read, it can never be left off. It is in that respect, we acknowledge, worse than port or brandy, which may be disused, though with great difficulty. But nobody is so melancholy as he who once takes in the Tatler and leaves it off. It is said that a Spanish king, observing one day a scholar reading a book on the banks of the Manzanares, and laughing as if he would kill himself, observed, "Either that young fellow is mad, or he is reading Don Quixote." Now on a similar principle, though by an illustration of it more painful, if you see a man walking by the side of a river, with a face betokening an intention of drowning himself, you may safely say "Either that man is mad, or he has left off his Tatler." The thing cannot be done with safety. The man becomes in the same state with Cardinal Richelieu, when he cut his facetious friend Boisrobert. The Cardinal consulted the physicians in vain. Nothing went well with him. Church and state had no longer any charms for him, nor courtiers, nor women, nor even the bad tragedies that he wrote. At length one of his medical advisers found out the secret, and left a prescription on his table to the following purport: "A dose of Boisrobert. Nothing else will do." The Cardinal renounced his Boisrobert, and recovered. Now we are a Boisrobert, with this difference, that our company is not confined to the service of cardinals, and that our cost is not to be thought of; whereas Boisrobert was an expensive fellow, and could not have enabled the Cardinal to relish his breakfast under some half-guinea a morning.

It would be superfluous to tell the *lawyers* that they must read us – at any rate the young lawyers. They have always been friends of wit and the drama; to say nothing of that universal knowledge which is necessary to prepare them against unexpected cases. It is a pity that for want of some proper periodical paper, like those which amused the Templars in the time of Steele and Addison, a cultivation of what might be called *town literature* has declined among the gentlemen of the Bar. A melancholy evidence of it was afforded the other day, when the rights of Mr. Arnold's licence were discussed before the Lord Chancellor. The old lawyers, on this occasion, betrayed a lamentable want of Tatlerism. Half-a-dozen of the youngest (we could mention their names) would have handled the question in so different a manner, that the ghost of Congreve and Wycherley (Templars) would have rejoiced; and visions of wits and perukes have been floating in the witness box.

Churchmen, in these dangerous times, should read us, in order that they may know what is thought of the church in all quarters, *Poets* must have us, because they must know everything, and also for the particular love we bear them; for which reasons *wits and philosophers* of all classes must be our friends. The *tradesman* ought to be our special friend, in order that he may vindicate the liberality of his tendencies, and shew how compatible prudence is with elegance of enjoyment. Some of the most extraordinary men in this country, the Defoes, the Richardsons, etc., have been tradesmen; and in Paris, where the wives and daughters oftener help in the shops than with us, nothing is more common than to see men and women take off their eyes from a book or a journal, and serve you with double alacrity from the refreshment. In Paris, they read even at the fruit-stalls (symptoms of which refinement of the pavé we have observed lately in our own metropolis); and we do not despair of a time before long, when a fair vender by the street-side, being asked how her "apples are today," shall say, looking up, and shewing a countenance as agreeable as what she sells, – "Pleasanter than ever, I think, Sir;" – fancying in her reverie over our pages, that the gentleman was asking how her Tatler was today.

As to *mechanics*, they have taken such a rise in the world of late, owing to the mighty power exhibited by their engines, and to the very poverty which has forced upon them a double portion of thought, that we are become almost as anxious to know what opinion a mechanic entertains of us, as a professed wit, or a leader of the town. This class has now periodical works of its own, institutions, lectures and what not; and we can hardly see one of the body; but we imagine we behold in him a future Dr. Franklin. If so, we are not afraid of him; for Franklin was a lover of pleasantry as well as science, of the humanities as well as the accomplishments of philosophy; and he contributed to periodical works himself, and would have written admirable Tatlers. We cannot help fancying the numerous proverbs which he and Swift would have poured forth, had they lived in these times, and witnessed all the information and entertainment we are diffusing at so cheap a rate. We cannot pretend to equal them in the masterly carelessness of that species of composition; but, as admirers of it, we may fancy that they might have condescended to some such golden sentences as the following: —

A Tatler a day is a library a year.

Take care of your Tatlers, and the volume will take care of itself.

> Early to breakfast, and Tatlers to read,
> Will make people healthy and wealthy indeed.

> When pence for buns are gone and spent,
> Then Tatlers are most excellent.

THE TATLER. NEW SERIES

APRIL, 1832

TO THE READER

The alteration of the size and shape of the *Tatler* having occasioned us, from accidental causes, more trouble than we anticipated, it is very probable that in this number some discrepancies may escape our notice, which will be remediable in future. For the rest, we are no friend to promises, which we have experienced to have affinity to pie-crust in other respects than their liability to be broken; for as pie-crust is pleasant to the palate, and afterwards but too often produces nightmare and indigestion; so do promises, made by the sanguine, and received by the expectants of good things with smiling countenances, issue not less often in regrets on the one part and reproaches on the other. Therefore it is that, sink or swim, we abstain from them; anticipating not the less to see the TATLER become better as it grows older; cultivating with effect the social feelings and abating asperity, which, by dividing attention, and diverting it from what should be its exclusive object, is continually hindering the progress of improvement. We profess to be single-minded and inflexible in these principles; and we expect, and indeed do not care to receive, support in their maintenance, but in proportion to the efficiency which is given to a work, whose scope is to recreate the minds of its readers with the salutary fruit of literature and the peaceful arts, leaving to others the more arduous task of warring with the enemies of general freedom, and through that of all the blessings consequent upon it.

LEIGH HUNT'S LONDON JOURNAL

To Assist the Enquiring, Animate the Struggling, and Sympathise with All

APRIL 2, 1834

ADDRESS

The object of this Publication, which is devoted entirely to subjects of miscellaneous interest, unconnected with politics, is to supply the lovers of knowledge, with an *English* Weekly Paper, similar in point of size and variety, to *Chambers's Edinburgh Journal*, but with a character a little more southern and literary. The acuteness and industry of the writers of the *Edinburgh Journal* are understood to have obtained a very large demand for their work; the illustrated information of the *Penny Magazine*, with its admirable wood-cuts, has obtained for it one still more stupendous; and though we may not be able to compete with either of these phenomena, and, indeed, are prepared to be content with a sale of reasonable enormity, yet there still remain gaps in the supplies of public intellect, which its consumers would willingly see filled up; and one of these we propose to accommodate. It may briefly be described as consisting in a want of something more connected with *the ornamental part of utility*, – with the art of extracting pleasurable ideas from the commonest objects, and the participations of a scholarly experience. In the metropolis there are thousands of improving and enquiring minds, capable of all the elegancies of intellectual enjoyment, who, for want of educations worthy of them, are deprived of a world of pleasures, in which they might have instructed others. We hope to be read by these. In every country town there is always a knot of spirits of this kind, generally young men, who are known, above others, for their love of books, for the liberality of their sentiments, and their desire to be acquainted with all that is going forward in connection with the graces of poetry and the fine arts. We hope to have *these* for our readers. Finally, almost every village has its cottagers of a similar tendency, who, notwithstanding their inferior opportunities, have caught from stray pieces of poetry and fiction, a sense of what their nature requires, in order to elevate its enjoyments or to console its struggles; and we trust we shall become the friends of these. In a word, (without meaning to disparage our excellent contemporaries, whose plans are of another sort, and have been most triumphantly borne out by success), as the *Edinburgh Journal* gives the world the benefit of its knowledge of business, and the *Penny Magazine* that of its authorities and its pictures, so the *London Journal* proposes to furnish ingenuous minds of all classes, with such helps as it possesses towards a share in the pleasures of taste and scholarship. For, to leave no class unspecified, it is not without the hope of obtaining the good-will of the highest of the well-educated, who love the very talk on such subjects, as they do that of a loving friend, apart from any want of his information, and who have been rendered too wise by their knowledge not to wish well to speculations which tend to do justice to all men, and to accompany the "march of intellect" with the music of kind thoughts.

It is proposed, as the general plan of the *Journal*, but not without the power of change or modification, as circumstances may suggest, that it should consist of One Original Paper or Essay every week, from the pen of the Editor; of matter combining entertainment with information, selected by him in the course of his reading, both old and new; of a weekly Abstract of some popular or otherwise interesting book, the spirit of which will be given *entire*, after the fashion of the excellent abridgments in *Johnstone's Edinburgh Magazine*; and, lastly, of a brief current notice of the Existing State of Poetry, Painting, and Music, and a general sprinkle of Notes, Verses, Miscellaneous Paragraphs, and other helps to pleasant and companionable perusal.

FURTHER REMARKS ON THE DESIGN OF THIS JOURNAL. POOR RICH MEN AND RICH POOR MEN. A WORD OR TWO ON THE PERIODICAL WRITINGS OF THE EDITOR

Pleasure is the business of this Journal: we own it: we love to begin it with the word: it is like commencing the day (as we are now commencing it) with sunshine in the room. Pleasure for all who can receive pleasure; consolation and encouragement for the rest; this is our device. But then it is pleasure like that implied by our simile, innocent, kindly, we dare to add, instructive and elevating. Nor shall the gravest aspects of it be wanting. As the sunshine floods the sky and the ocean, and yet nurses the baby buds of the roses on the wall, so we would fain open the largest and the very least sources of pleasure, the noblest that expands above us into the heavens, and the most familiar that catches our glance in the homestead. We would break open the surfaces of habit and indifference, of objects that are supposed to contain nothing but so much brute matter, or common-place utility, and show what treasures they conceal. Man has not yet learnt to en-joy the world he lives in; no, not the hundred-thousand-mil-lionth part of it; and we would fain help him to render it productive of still greater joy, and to delight or comfort him-self in his task as he proceeds. We would make adversity hopeful, prosperity sympathetic, all kinder, richer, and happier. And we have some right to assist in the endeavour, for there is scarcely a single joy or sorrow within the experience of our fellow-creatures which we have not tasted; and the belief in the good and beautiful has never forsaken us. It has been medicine to us in sickness, riches in poverty, and the best part of all that ever delighted us in health and success.

There is not a man living perhaps in the present state of society, – certainly not among those who have a surfeit of goods, any more than those who want a sufficiency, – that has not some pain which he would diminish, and some pleasure, or capability of it, that he would increase. We would say to him, let him be sure he can diminish that pain and increase that pleasure. He will find out the secret, by knowing more, and by knowing that there is more to love. "Pleasures lie about our feet." We would extract some for the unthinking rich man out of his very carpet, (though he thinks he has already got as much as it can yield) ; and for the unthinking or unhoping poor one, out of his bare floor.

"Can you put a loaf on my table?" the poor man may ask. No: but we can show him how to get it in the best manner, and comfort himself while he is getting it. If he can get it not at all, we do not profess to have even the right of being listened to by him. We can only do what we can, as his fellow-creatures, and by other means, towards hastening the termination of so frightful an exception to the common lot.

"Can you rid me of my gout, or my disrelish of all things?" the rich man may ask. No: nor perhaps even diminish it, unless you are a very daring or a very sensible man; and if you are very rich indeed, and old, neither of these predicaments is very likely. Yet we would try. We are inextinguishable friends of endeavour.

If you had the gout, however, *and were Lord Holland*, you would smile and say, "Talk on." You would suspend the book, or the pen, or the kindly thought you were engaged in, and indulgently wait to see what recipes or amusing fancies we could add to your stock.

Nay, if you were a kind of starving Dr. Johnson, who wrote a letter one day to the editor of the magazine to which he contributed, signing himself, "Dinnerless," [1] you would listen to us, even without a loaf on your table, and see how far we could bear out the reputation of the Lydians, who are said to have invented play as a resource against hunger. But Dr. Johnson knew he had his remedy in his wits. The wants of the poor in knowledge are not so easily postponed. With deep reverence and sympathy would we be understood as speaking of them. A smile, however closely it may border upon a grave thought, is not to be held a levity in us, any more than sun betwixt rain. One and the same sympathy with all things, fetches it out.

But to all but the famished we should say, with the noble text, "Man does not live by bread alone." "A man," says Bacon, in words not unworthy to go by the side of the others, "is but what he knoweth." "I think," said Descartes; "therefore I am." A man has no proof of his existence but in his consciousness of it, and the return of that consciousness after sleep. He is therefore, in *amount* of existence, only so much as his consciousness, his thoughts, and his feelings amount to. The more he knows, the more he exists; and the pleasanter his knowledge, the happier his existence. One man, in this sense of things, and it is a sense proved beyond a doubt, (except with those merry philosophers of antiquity who doubted their very consciousness, nay, doubted doubt itself), is infinitely little compared with another man. If we could see his

---

[1] *Impransus.* It might mean simply, that he had not dined; but there is too much reason to believe otherwise. And yet how much good and entertainment did not the very necessities of such a man help to produce us!

mind, we should see a pigmy; and it would be stuck perhaps into a pint of beer, or a scent-bottle, or a bottle of wine; as the monkey stuck Gulliver into the marrow-bone. Another man's mind would show larger; another larger still; till at length we should see minds of all shapes and sizes, from a microscopic body to that of a giant or a demi-god, or a spirit that filled the visible world. Milton's would be like that of his own archangel. "His stature reached the sky." Shakespeare's would stretch from the midst of us into the regions of "airy nothing," and bring us new creatures of his own making. Bacon's would be lost into the next ages. Many a "great man's" would become invisible; and many a litttle one suddenly astonish us with the overshadowing of his greatness.

Men sometimes, by the magic of their knowledge, partake of a great many things which they do not possess: others possess much which is lost upon them. It is recorded of an *exquisite*, in one of the admirable exhibitions of Mr. Mathews, that being told, with a grave face, of a mine of silver which had been discovered in one of the London suburbs, he exclaimed, in his jargon, "A mine of *sil-vau*! Good *Gaud*! You don't tell me so! A mine of *sil-vau*; Good *Gaud*! I've often seen the little boys playing about, but I had no idea that there was a mine of *sil-vau*."

This gentleman, whom we are to understand as repeating these words out of pure ignorance and absurdity, and not from any power to receive information, would be in possession, while he was expressing his astonishment at a thing unheard of and ridiculous, of a hundred real things round about him, of which he knew nothing. Shakspeare speaks of a man who was "incapable of his own distress;" that is to say, who had not the feelings of other men, and was insensible to what would have distressed everybody else. This *dandy* would be incapable of his own wealth, of his own furniture, of his own health, friends, books, gardens; nay of his very hat and coat, except inasmuch as they contributed to give him one single idea; to wit, that of his *dandyism*. From all those stores, small and great, nothing but that solitary and sorry impression would he receive.

Of all which his wealth could procure him, in the shape of a real enjoyment of poetry, paintings, music, sculpture, and the million of ideas which they might produce, he would know nothing.

Of all the countries that produced his furniture, all the trades that helped to make it, all the arts that went to adorn it, all the materials of which it was composed, and the innumerable images of men, lands, faculties, substances, elements, and interesting phenomena of all sorts to which the knowledge might give rise, he would know nothing.

Of his books he would know nothing, except that they were bound, and that they *caust* a great deal.

Of his gardens he would know nothing, except that they were "tedious," and that he occasionally had a pink out of them to put in his button-hole – provided it was the fashion. Otherwise pinks are "vulgar." Nature's and God's fashion is nothing.

Of his hat and his coat it might be thought he must know something; but he would not, except as far as we have stated; – unless, indeed, his faculties might possibly attain to the knowledge of a "fit" or a "set," and then he would not know it with a grace. The knowledge of a good thing, even in the least matters, is not for a person so poorly educated – so worse than left to grow up in an ignorance unsophisticate. Of the creatures that furnished the materials of his hat and coat, – the curious handicraft beaver, the spinster silk-worm, the sheep in the meadows (except as mutton), nothing would he know, or care, or receive the least pleasurable thought from. In the mind that constitutes *his* man – in the amount of *his* existence – terribly vacant are the regions – bald places in the map – desarts without even the excitement of a storm. Nothing lives there but himself – a suit of clothes in a solitude – emptiness in emptiness.

Contrast a being of this fashion (after all allowance for caricature) with one who has none of his deformities, but with a stock of ideas such as the other wants. Suppose him poor, even struggling, but not unhappy; or if not without unhappiness, yet not without relief, and unacquainted with the desperation of the other's ennui. Such a man, when he wants recreation for his thoughts, can make them flow from all the objects, or the ideas of those objects, which furnish nothing to the other. The commonest goods and chattels are pregnant to him as fairy tales, or things in a pantomime. His hat, like Fortunatus's Wishing Cap, carries him into the American solitudes among the beavers, where he sits in thought, looking at them during their work, and hearing the majestic whispers in the trees, or the falls of the old trunks that are everlastingly breaking the silence in those wildernesses. His coat shall carry him, in ten minutes, through all the scenes of pastoral life and mechanical, the quiet fields, the sheep-shearing, the feasting, the love-making, the downs of Dorsetshire and the streets of Birmingham, where if he meet with pain in his sympathy, he also, in his knowledge, finds reason for hope and encouragement, and for giving his manly assistance to the common good. The very tooth-pick of the *dandy*, should this man, or any man like him meet with it, poor or rich, shall suggest to him, if he pleases, a hundred agreeable thoughts of foreign lands, and elegance and amusement, – of tortoises and books of travels, and the comb in his mistress's hair, and the elephants that carry sultans, and the real silver mines of Potosi, with all the wonders of South American history, and the starry cross in its sky; so that the smallest key shall pick the lock of the greatest treasures; and that which in the hands of the possessor was only a poor instrument of affectation, and the very emblem of indifference and stupidity, shall open to the knowing man a universe.

We must not pursue the subject further this week, or trust our eyes at the smallest objects around us, which, from long and loving contemplation, have enabled us to report their riches. We have been at this work now, off and on, man and boy, (for we began essay-writing while in our teens), for upwards of thirty years; and excepting that, we would fain have done far more, and that experience and suffering have long restored to us the natural kindliness of boyhood, and put an end to a belief in the right or utility of severer views of any thing or person, we feel the same as we have done throughout; and we have the same hope, the same love, the same faith in the beauty and goodness of nature and all her prospects, in space and in time; we could almost add, if a sprinkle of white hairs in our black would allow us, the same youth; for whatever may be thought of a consciousness to that effect, the feeling is so real, and trouble of no ordinary kind has so remarkably spared the elasticity of our spirits, that we are often startled to think how old we have become, compared with the little of age that is in our disposition: and we mention this to bespeak the reader's faith in what we shall write hereafter, if he is not acquainted with us already. If he is, he will no more doubt us than the children do at our fireside. We have had so much sorrow, and yet are capable of so much joy, and receive pleasure from so many familiar objects, that we sometimes think we should have had an unfair portion of happiness, if our life had not been one of more than ordinary trial.

The reader will not be troubled in future with personal intimations of this kind; but in commencing a new work of the present nature and having been persuaded to put our name at the top of it, (for which we beg his kindest constructions, as a point conceded by a sense of what was best for others), it will be thought, we trust, not unfitting in us to have alluded to them. We believe we may call ourselves the father of the present penny and three half-penny literature, — designations, once distressing to "ears polite," but now no longer so, since they are producing so many valuable results, fortunes included. The first number of the new popular review, the *Printing Machine*, in an article for the kindness and cordiality of which we take this our best opportunity of expressing our gratitude, and can only wish we could turn these sentences into so many grips of the hand to show our sense of it, — did us the honour of noticing the *Indicator* as the first successful attempt (in one respect) to revive something like the periodical literature of former days. We followed this with the *Companion*, lately republished in connection with the *Indicator*; and a few years ago, in a fit of anxiety at not being able to meet some obligations, and fearing we were going to be cut off from life itself without leaving answers to still graver wants, we set up a half-reviewing, half-theatrical periodical, under the name of the *Tatler,* (a liberty taken by love), in the hope of being able to realize some sudden as well as lasting profits! So little, with all our zeal for the public welfare, had we found out what was so well discerned by Mr. Knight and others, when they responded to the intellectual wants of the *many*. However, we pleased some readers, whom it is a kind of prosperity even to rank as such: we conciliated the good-will of others, by showing that an ardent politician might still be a man of no ill-temper, nor without good-will to all; and now, once more setting up a periodical work, entirely without politics, but better calculated, we trust, than our former ones to meet the wishes of many as well as few, we are in hearty good earnest, the public's very sincere and cordial friend and servant,

LEIGH HUNT

THE LONDON JOURNAL

WEDNESDAY, APRIL 23, 1834

Having arrived at the fourth number of our Journal, with the most encouraging prospects of success, we must leave off saying what heaps of kind letters we continue to receive, lest it should look like a system of self-recommendation. But we cannot help once more alluding to them, for fear of seeming ungrateful to the writers; some of whom are as flattering to us by their very names, as all are by their cordiality. One letter, however, is of a nature so publicly as well as privately connected with the subject of a journal of this description, that we must take the liberty, not only of distinctly mentioning it, but of laying it before the reader. We own, that after our first impulse to this effect, we hesitated a moment out of feelings of modesty, and somewhat longer in deference to that of the writer, especially as he had given no intimation whether we might so use it or not. Our mind was soon made up by the consideration of the honour which the letter did him, and of the good which must accrue to the public from seeing men, who might be supposed to witness a new Journal of this sort with no friendly feeling, coming forward in so handsome a manner to shew themselves true lovers of the knowledge they advocate, and of the generosities to which it gives rise. Mr. Chambers may over-estimate our abilities, and be too modest respecting his own; but there can only be one opinion respecting the sentiment that impelled him to write his letter. He will be glad to hear, that it is not the first of this kind which we have received. We take the opportunity of stating, that no sooner had our Journal appeared, than the Publisher of the *Penny Magazine*, who is also, we believe, proprietor of the *Printing Machine*, or *Review for the Many*, expressed himself in the most spirited and liberal manner towards the new paper, and took steps to shew that he was in earnest. But Mr. Chambers has written so much at length on the subject, that we feel warranted in calling the reader's attention to his letter, and we think we cannot do better than put it in this part of our Journal, where we are in the habit of noticing any new evidences that transpire, of the growth of intellectual brotherhood : —

LETTER OF MR. ROBERT CHAMBERS OF THE EDINBURGH JOURNAL TO THE EDITOR OF THE LONDON JOURNAL

"27, Elder-Street, Edinburgh
"April 15, 1834.

"Dear Sir, — I take leave to address you in this familiar manner for several reasons. The chief is your kind nature, as exemplified in your writings, which prove you the friend of all mankind; the lesser are your allusions on more occasions than one to writings of mine, when you did not perhaps know the exact name of the author. My purpose is to congratulate you on the first number of your Journal, which I have just seen, and to express my earnest and sincere hope that it will repay your exertions, and render the latter part of your life more prosperous than you say the earlier has been. You will perhaps appreciate my good wishes the more that they proceed from an individual who, according to vulgar calculations, might expect to be injured by your success. I assure you, so far from entertaining any grudge towards your work on that score, I am as open to receive pleasurable impressions from it as I have ever been from your previous publications, or as the least literary of your readers can be; and as hopeful that it will succeed and prove a means of comfort to you, as the most ancient and familiar of your friends. I know that your work can never do by a tenth part so much ill to my brother and myself, as it may do good to you — for every book, however similar to others, finds in a great measure new channels for itself; and still more certain am I, that the most jealous and unworthy feelings we could entertain, would be ineffectual in protecting us from the consequences of your supplanting our humble sheets in the public favour. My brother and I feel much pleasure in observing that a writer so much our senior, and so much our superior, should have thought our plan to such an extent worthy of his adoption, and hope your doing so will only furnish additional proof of the justice of our calculations. This leads me to remark, that, while I acknowledge the truth of your pretensions to having been the reviver of the periodical literature of a former age, and have looked to your manner of treating light subjects as in part the model of our own, I must take this and every other proper opportunity of asserting my elder brother's merit, as the originator of cheap respectable publications, of the class to which your Journal is so important an addition. In the starting of *Chambers's Edinburgh Journal* in February, 1832, he was unquestionably the first to develope this new power of the printing-press; and, considering that we had some little character (at least in Scotland) to lose, and encountered feelings in our literary brethren little less apt, I may say, to deter us from our object than the terrors which assailed Rodolph in the Witch's Glen (a simile more expressive than it is apt), I humbly conceive that, when the full utility of my brother's invention shall have been perceived by the world, as I trust it will in time, he will be fully entitled to have his claims allowed without dispute.

"That we have regretted to find ourselves the objects of so many of the meaner order of feelings among our brethren, it would be vain to deny. I must say, however, that we would have been ill to satisfy indeed, if the admission of our weekly sheet into almost every family of the middle rank, and many of the lower throughout the country, had not more than compensated us for that affliction. Our labours, moreover, are profitable beyond our hopes, beyond our wants, besides yielding to us a ceaseless revenue of pleasure, in the sense they convey to us of daily and hourly improving the hearts and understandings of a large portion of our species. That you may aim as heartily at this result, and be as successful in obtaining it, is the wish of

"Dear Sir,

"Your sincere Friend and Servant,

"Robert Chambers"

We shall add nothing to this, being naturally willing to leave Mr. Chambers in possession of his pleasant "last word," except that the appearance of the *Tatler* was antecedent to that of the *Edinburgh Journal*, and that in the *Indicator*, and in the *Tatler* also, (if we recollect rightly), we professed a wish to extend an acquaintance with matters of intellectual refinement among the uneducated. The zeal of our correspondent, however, in behalf of his brother's claim, is so good a thing for its own sake, that we are far from anxious to contest this point with him; and heartily willing are we to acknowledge, that these gentlemen have had a wider and more popular view of the opening of cheap literature to the many, than we ever had till now. In zeal for the interests of all, we will yield to nobody; but in a knowledge of the best means of extending its operation, others have surpassed us; and we hope to shew, that we have profited by their example. We take this opportunity of observing, that among the foremost, if not the very first, to lower the price of respectable periodical literature, though not professedly to extend it to those who have missed a classical education, was the *Athenæum*.

LEIGH HUNT'S LONDON JOURNAL

WEDNESDAY, JUNE 25, 1834

UNSOCIAL READERS OF PERIODICALS

Dear *Quondam* Indicator,

That which I have so long desired, is at length accomplished; — I mean your return to us in the hebdomadal way, which in by-gone days afforded both pleasure and instruction to so many circles. But wherefore have you changed the size of your sheet? Fifteen years since, when sitting at the tea-table with your paper, I have imagined myself one, living in the *"queen's time,"* whose taste was directed and conserved by an Addison. The lapse of years has not impaired the character of the Indicator with me, and I have a sensible gratification in the prospect of a renewal of those times. This change in the form is however, some drawback, and is to me twofold. First, inasmuch as the illusion is weakened; — and secondly, which is yet more tantalizing. . . . But the "second count" involves a narrative, which shall be unfolded with all brevity, and to which you are invited most graciously to lend an ear.

Imprimis, I wish you would not place *Leigh Hunt* at the head of your Journal; I would still call you, *"dear Indicator;"* but no matter for the name. Now to the narrative. Know then, that I am the wife of a gentleman, remarkable for the regularity of his habits, on which he plumes himself not a little. Having a taste for purchasing most of the periodicals, he stitches together all those, which from their similarity in size, are susceptible of this conjunction. Thus, when I would be *tête-à-tête* with you, "Chambers's Information for the People," presents itself; and what is more, the sheet must always be appended to those miscellanies, ere it be consigned to me. The octavo would not have been liable to this accident, there being no work of that form going on at this time in weekly succession.

This is one of the many annoyances arising out of the love of *order*; a superstition (when it amounts to such) to which *you*, as a party concerned, would do well to apply your ingenuity in the exposure of its inconvenience. "The inconvenience of order!" some would exclaim. To such I would not address myself. There is no one to whom I would consign the handling a paradox, with such confidence, as to you. Twenty years long have I borne that *The Examiner* should be cut and sewed before it was resigned to one, out of four or five, who waited in vain for a sheet. Need I point out to you the comfort of holding a page of a favourite author between the fire and your eyes; with your feet placed on the fender; contrasted with being planted at a large table, remote from such appliances, and sitting bolt upright as though you were examining Magna Charta! I hope you will think of some alleviation to a lone family, living in the country, where to read is almost the only resource, and where any abridgement of this pleasure is a serious annoyance. One thing I do insist on, that you turn not the shafts of your wit against us. We look to you for succor. We hear a vast deal of the *"ignorant impatience"* of women, and the necessity of restraining it; and if *you, too*, were to glance that way, it would be the *unkindest cut of all*. But we know you for a 'Squire of Dames. *En passant*, an occasional Essay in support of our claims to a small share of understanding, would not be misplaced. Your late friend Hazlitt took some pains to prove, that women were totally incapable of reasoning; and it must be acknowledged that he had reason for the assertion. I never knew any woman, nor man either, save one or two fantastical wits, who could develop the mysteries of his ratiocinations. But *de mortuis* &c. I shall look with no small trepidation for recognition of our grievances; and do engage, in case they are *properly noticed*, to furnish such remuneration, as may amply reward a man of letters and an elegant poet. Imprimis, in the village of *Mopeham*, where I reside, (it is not *that Mopeham* where dwells the old lady of oblivious memory; and from whence the "Parson's Daughter" posted home in the carriage *tête-à-tête* with the young Count. This was thought, in our circle, rather a new incident, and a happy hit in the *novel* department). But to leave digression: this Mopeham is *Our Village*; and in its woody haunts are to be found more nightingales than, perchance, you may have ever heard or seen congregate; for you see them in their flight from one tree to another throughout the day "when every goose is cackling," yet lose they none of their fame as *prima donnas*. Now do I intend noting every minim, crochet, quaver, &c. &c. in the combined scale of harmony, to present you with; and yet this is only a small part of what I project, if you will undertake to prove that *order* does *not always* produce harmony; and to disabuse, of that other heresy, one, on whom time has no other effect than to strengthen and confirm him in preconceived errors.

It was with much concern I read in your commencement to your present work, that you should cease to speak of yourself in future. There has been a long hiatus in our acquaintance, and I had hoped to have collected some gleanings from your hearth again, — that hearth which I used to picture as the union of what was most pleasing and elegant. You once wrote, long ago, that in the contemplation of a Poet's honeymoon there was more of speculation than in the moons of common mortals; and the sequel, in that instance, strengthened your hypothesis. But hearths change; blooming children become men and women, having the same wants as ourselves, which we are not so ready to accord to them; they murmur, and often with reason. There is much difficulty in abstracting from the mind the impression that they are still but children. But I must conclude; for this subject will lead me beyond my limits; so I finish with expressing a hope that these changes may have fallen lightly on one, who has been so much the favourite of nature, that fortune, in her envy of his endowments, has been oft unwilling to recognise the justice of his claims.

Pardon must be asked for the loose half sheet, with which this letter commences. It had been written on the other side, before the mistake was discovered.

Vale!
Griselda.

Mopeham, May-day, (Incongruous!) 1834.

TO OUR READERS
AUGUST 13, 1834

Since the publication of the first number of our Journal, we have had a succession of letters from different quarters, recommending us to give up our page of Advertisements, as tending to do it less good than harm, and defacing the future volume. The reasons which existed for declining this advice, exist no longer; and we are accordingly happy to gratify our friends by giving up the page, and chatting with them to the last drop of our ink.

OBJECTS OF THE LONDON JOURNAL
SEPTEMBER 3, 1834

Montaigne says, that he delights to ring the word "pleasure" in the ears of philosophers who affect to despise it, and who are as fond of it as any men, after their fashion. Since the setting up of this cheerful and most Christian journal, we have known but two instances of objection to it; and to these we answer, that the very grounds of their objection are those which have procured us two hundred approbations. One of these objections was in a criticism, begging us not to "affect" so much sentiment (as if, because the *writer* would have "affected" so much, had he shewn it, that therefore *we* did); — the other implied that we were invariably too pleased, and with not enough reason, — that we fetched our satisfaction out of too many common things, and did not succeed after all. For the success, we can luckily refer to other readers: and as to the rest, it was our plan and system, and forms the very essence, utility, and prosperity of our journal. Our object was to put more sunshine into the feelings of our countrymen, more good will and good humour, a greater *habit* of being pleased with one another and with everything, and therefore a greater power of dispensing with uneasy sources of satisfaction. We wished to create one corner and field of periodical literature, in which men might be sure of hope and cheerfulness, and of the cultivation of peaceful and flowery thoughts, without the accompaniment of anything inconsistent with them; we knew that there was a desire at the bottom of every human heart to retain a faith in such thoughts, and to see others believe in the religion and recommend it; and heartily have anxious as well as happy readers in this green and beautiful England responded to our belief. We condemn no other publication, conducted honestly, on different principles. There is a noble as well as ignoble warfare, and the time for either, for aught we know, may not have gone by. We condemn none of the mysterious struggles of humanity, even the most passionate, some of them perhaps nobler and more necessary than our ceasing to struggle in that sort; on the contrary, in "sympathizing with all," how can we leave them out? But, as far as our own system of action goes, we may be allowed to cultivate a variety of endeavor, if it be only *as* a variety, and to confine ourselves to the hope of winning and persuading. There are green fields in the world, as well as fields of battle; and in making a grove, or a park, or other domestic elysium, people do not contemplate the introduction in it of fight and contest and sour speeches. A man may say if he pleases, "I cannot live in your peaceful grounds, with their trees and sunshine, where all which is alive is happy or comforted, and the tragedies are nothing but old stories: I must go and get up a sensation at the police office, or the hospital, or the butcher's, or read a lampoon, or some writing worse than my own, or get up a superiority to somebody somehow, in order to keep myself in heart with myself." Let him go. Nay, we will go with him, provided he will let us find things to be a little better than he takes them for, even himself; for the reader will bear us witness that we avoid no places for their homeliness, and can vindicate the supposed "weed" as well as the accepted flower. But it does not follow that our ground is not a good ground, for all this; or that people have not reason to like it; especially as they are apt to have troubles enough elsewhere, and all but the very restless or thoughtless like to have some sequestered spot to repose in, — personally, if they can get it, — mentally, if they have not wealth or leisure enough, or a green neighbourhood. The *London Journal* is a sort of park for rich and poor, for the reflecting and well intentioned of all sorts; where every one can be alone, or in company, as he thinks fit, and see, with his mind's eye, a succession of Elysian sights, ancient and modern, and as many familiar objects to boot, or hear nothing but birds and waterfalls or the comforted beatings of his own heart, — all effected for him by no greater magician than Good Faith and a little reading. Good Faith is his host, and Reading the page that brings books to his host; and Love has ordained that Good Faith, and a little reading, shall be able to do such wonders for us as reading's biggest brothers with no faith at all, shall have no notion of. Children and men co-exist in the world; and the child and the man must co-exist in the little world of man's individuality, in order that he may see at once manfully and with delight. "Except ye become as little children," &c. We would not lightly apply so great a text; but the greatness of the text includes every degree of loving applicability; and as there is nothing in the world which is not supernatural in one sense, – as the very world of fashion itself rolls round with the stars, and is a part of the mystery and the variety of the shews of the universe, – so nothing, in a contemptuous sense, is small, or unworthy of a grave and calm hope, which tends to popularize Christian refinement, and to mix it up with every species of social intercourse, as a good realized, and not merely as an abstraction preached. What! Have not philosophy and christianity long since met, in the embrace of such loving discoveries? And do not the least and most trivial things, provided they have an earnest and cheerful good will, partake of some right of greatness, and the privilege to be honoured? if not with admiration of their wisdom, yet with acknowledgment of the joy which is the end of wisdom, and which it is the privilege of a loving sincerity to reach by a short road. Hence we have had two objections, and two hundred encouragements; and excellent writers of all sorts, and of all other shades of belief, have hastened to say to us, "Preach that, and prosper."

Have not the *Times*, and the *Examiner*, and the *Atlas*, and the *Albion*, and the *True Sun*, and twenty other newspapers, hailed us for the very sunniness of our religion? Does not that old and judicious Whig, the *Scotsman*, waive his deliberate manner in our favour, and "cordially" wish us success for it? Does not the radical *Glasgow Argus*, in an eloquent article, "fresh and glowing" as his good will, expressly recommend us for its pervading all we write upon, tears included? And the rich-writing Tory, Christopher North, instead of objecting to the entireness of our sunshine, and requiring a cloud in it, does he not welcome it, aye, every week, as it strikes on his breakfast-cloth and speak of it in a burst of bright-heartedness; as "dazzling the snow?"

Of a truth, it would not be difficult for us, old soldiers as we are, and accustomed to rougher labours in former times, to summon up a little of our old battle-grip, and lay a young gentleman or so double on the green sward, after the fashion of Entellus or Abraham Cann. Easily could we take him in hand, and lift him off his ground, and lock up his meditated "fibbing," and so trussing head and heels together, make a soft present of him to his mother earth. But *cui bono*? Where would be the good of it, even to himself? And why hurt the better use of his faculties, which we hope he will turn to handsomer account? Has not every man and every cause, in this imperfect state of things, a side on which he or it may be assailed, so far as to make him ridiculous (if there is the wit to do it) or uncomfortable, or to vex or injure him in some way or other? And shall we violate our principles, even out of resentment, and join in keeping up so old a story, and (as it appears to us) so useless a ground of re-action, — helping to sow new hostilities, by very reason of our objecting to old? Not we. We are willing to be differed with to whatever honest extreme, and to answer, as well as we can, all objections, which we have no reason to believe disingenuous; but nothing but a matter of life and death to our Journal shall induce us to be hostile with anybody; and after these announcements, coupled with the hazards of all sorts which we have encountered in old times, we think it will be held something a little worse than superfluous to assail us after a hostile fashion. We are at peace with all; and as we seek the common good, and sail under white banners, we gladly receive the encouragement, and feel ourselves under the protection of all who honestly pursue it, even by rougher means. It is not of endeavourers such as we are, without arms, insulting nobody, and offending no public manners, that generous warriors will make an exception to their letters of license.

Still blow then, ye fair winds, and keep open upon us, ye blue heavens, – or rather, still shine in the whiteness of thy intention, thou fair flag, even against the blackest cloud, and still hail us as ye go, all gallant brother voyagers, and encourage us to pursue the kindly task which Love and Adversity have taught us, touching at all curious shores of reality and romance, endeavouring to make them know and love one another, to learn what is good against the roughest elements, or how the suffering that cannot be remedied may be best endured, to bring news of hope and joy and exaltation from the wings of the morning and the uttermost parts of the sea, making familiar companions, but not the less revered on that account, of the least things on earth and the greatest things apart from it, – of the dust and the globe, and the divided moon, of sun and stars, and the loneliest meetings of man's thought with immensity, which is not too large for his heart, though it be for his knowledge, because knowledge is but man's knowledge, but the heart has a portion of God's wisdom, which is love.

Have we none but bright subjects to talk of? No: no more than the sun-beam strikes upon none but bright objects, though it helps to make them bright. But may we not shine, if we can, upon the dullest, and show there is more in it than the dull suspect? May we not shine upon coldness, and warm it? Upon sorrow, and comfort it? May we not also endeavour to add confidence to joy, and show it how rich it is in the commonest coin of the visible? And is not this, instead of confining ourselves to one view of anything, not rather throwing the universal light of day (hitherto insufficiently valued) upon objects of all sorts, not excepting the darkest as well as the commonest? Does the human heart, in its struggles, require such comfort or does it not? And is not its comfort extended (at least with all minds wise enough to be generous, and to know a good when they see it) by the very sight of so much belief in good, especially when unconquered by suffering?

We trust, that as this is the first, so it will be the last time we shall think it advisable to touch upon a point that forces us upon one of those appearances of egotism, which the egotistical are so ready to denounce; but as we have really no misgivings about the matter, we shall conclude this article, while we are about it, with some beautiful and affecting verses which have been addressed to us, and which have seasonably arrived to contribute to that very confidence, which, on any other occasion perhaps they might have dashed: for the praise from a friend, which is triumphantly seized upon as a shield against objection, might well beget a blushing doubt if only worn as an ornament. But see how little this gentleman, who is one of the most accomplished persons of our acquaintance, a wit, a scholar, and a musician, doubts the desirableness of our mode of conveying comfort; and with what instinctive beauty, like the flowers of which he writes, his thoughts issue out of their dark ground, and climb upon the stalk of their natural ascendancy, and stand in consummate elegance, giving out the fragrance of their hearts, and looking with pensive superiority upon the earth from which they rose. Great, unquestionably, are his troubles, greater, in some respects, from the very prime of his life, and from the natural and acquired advantages he possesses; but assuredly the greater will be his triumph over them; for is he not able to bring beauty out of sorrow, to seize the smallest occasions for the greatest comfort, and to gather to him the hearts of his friends in sympathy and in zeal? It has been observed of the deaf, that they are not apt to be so cheerful as the blind;

and it is true, and for an obvious reason. Being able to help themselves on many occasions, they are too much left to shift for themselves on all, and are thus too often deprived of the sweetest advantage of society, conversation; whereas, the blind man, helpless in all other respects, is helped not only to a double portion of that one, but to a ten-fold measure of love and service at all times. Let him keep it in God's name, and repay us twenty fold with the delight of his blind eyes. But as deaf men, for these most pardonable reasons, are apt to be caustic and resentful, so we know not a more amiable sight on earth, than one, who in requiring a good measure of this help to consolation, cultivates the graces of patience and the willingness to be pleased, and without affecting to be insensible to his evils, turns them into attractions of love and reverence, and takes out of the endeavour to entertain him all pain, but that of not being able to convince him that he does not give any. It is true, in the instance before us, as much entertainment is brought, as can be received, and the merit is thus lessened as far as a consciousness to that effect cannot but prevail over an undue modesty. Nor, considering his good faith in all other respects, do we despair of convincing our friend that he has no reason to doubt any one's gladness to reciprocate entertainment with him. But we are keeping our readers from better things than prose. We make no apology of any general sort for publishing the verses, because, setting aside even their merit as such, we take them to be high evidences of the good which the design of this journal is doing with all ingenuous readers, and because the extension of a common sympathy, on any just ground whatsoever, is one of its main objects.

[The verses which follow are, in fact, rather weakly sentimental. – ED.]

NOTICE TO THE PUBLIC

IMPROVEMENTS OF THE "LONDON JOURNAL" FOR THE ENSUING YEAR

DECEMBER 17, 1834

As all Periodicals, at the commencement of a new year, must desire to obtain fresh readers, and show regard to old ones, by as much improvement or novelty as they can devise, and as we have no inclination to be behind-hand with our contemporaries in evincing either our zeal or gratitude, we hereby give a foretaste of our proper Journal pretensions, by setting modesty utterly aside; and do fairly acknowledge, that on Wednesday, the 7th of January next, we mean to be extremely brilliant and astonishing.

It is of no use to mince the matter. If we have been good hitherto we mean to be twenty-fold better then. If people (particularly those of a lofty five-shilling turn of mind) have been hitherto astonished how we could sell our weekly stores of knowledge and entertainment for the unmentionable sum of three half-pence, they shall then be amazed beyond endurance. Men shall be found, with our Journal in their hands, staring and immovable, under peril of a locked-jaw; while the fair sex, with a sweeter access of frenzy, and agreeable to their more patient endurance of a transport, yet not knowing withal how to express their satisfaction, shall be tempted literally to devour our pages, – perhaps in a sandwich, as Miss Catherine Fisher, out of a less exalted feeling, did the banknote.

Good heavens! if all our contemporaries improve as we do, what a periodical literature we shall have! The old "Gentleman's Magazine," their father, will be so very old and very gentlemanly, that nothing will ever have been seen so venerable, not even his churches. "Blackwood" will be so intense,

that there will be no distinguishing him from the woods and
fountains he speaks of. His magazine, coming to us, overshadowing, will be like a visit from the clouds and mountain
tops of the primeval world; or of Greece with all its isles.
"Tait" and the "Monthly Repository" will blow such notes
of advancement, that we shall all of a sudden be living in the
twenty-first century, all thriving and merry, our days cut
beautifully in two betwixt work and leisure. "Fraser" will
bring English orthodoxy so well acquainted with Irish and
French vivacity, that all three shall be astonished at finding
themselves shaking hands over Rabelais' "Oracle of the Bottle." The "New Monthly" shall be so very polite and "dis-
tingué," that men shall put a leaf of it into their button holes
instead of myrtle. The "Metropolitan" shall begin a new
novel once a month, and render us so jolly and maritime
that, like the drinkers in the "Naufragium Joculare," we
shall take our room for a ship and begin tossing the furniture
out of window to lighten her. Then the orthodox "Dublin
University Magazine" shall more and more delight the "candid reader" by praising Whigs who write about forest-trees
and Radicals who can relish claret. All war, in short, shall
become, in a manner, all peace, — the war being only a sort of
robust joviality, — a Donny-brook fair, — to relish the peace
with; and peaceful magazines shall, of course, have a prodigious deal to do. Mr. Loudon, with his "Architectural," "Gar-
dening," and "Naturalist's" Magazines, shall build all our
houses for us, plant all our gardens, and illustrate all our
fields.

By the way, what have we done, that the "Monthly Repository" has not been sent us, ever since we made an extract
from it? And how is it, that "Tait" and "Blackwood" are not
sent, as they used to be when we wrote in another Journal?
Our universalities, we are sure, do not offend them. They are
too much in earnest themselves, and, agreeably to the inso-

lence of our companionship, we must remind them of an anecdote in Boswell. Johnson dined one day in company with Wilkes, at Dilly's, the bookseller in the Poultry. There was a coldness at first; but wine, wit, and natural humanity, fused all parties together before dinner was over; and Wilkes, leaning back in his chair, and speaking to some one behind Johnson's back, said, in a stage-whisper, "I understand Dr. Johnson has written a very fine book (the 'Lives of the Poets'); but I am a poor patriot, and have not been able to see it." "Mr. Dilly," said Johnson, smiling with benignity (as Boswell says), "be good enough to send a copy of the 'Lives' to Mr. Wilkes." Now we have no ambition to compare ourselves with Wilkes, except inasmuch as he desired the public welfare (if he did); but we may be allowed, without any immodesty, to measure our inability to buy books with an Alderman and Member of Parliament; and "candid readers" are deserving the consideration of good editors.

To return to our subjèct; – we propose, in our next year's Journal, in addition to most of the features of the year past, to give regular notices of the Fine Arts and Music; a Memoir (every week) of some eminent person, taken from some good author; regular extracts from good books of Travels, so that the reader may go round the world with us in the course of the twelvemonth; specimens, also (we hope) of the best English Poets; and a sprinkle of more original matter, generally. And the proprietors of "Mr: Hazlitt's Characters of Shakspeare's Plays" (which are out of print) have kindly permitted us to promise one of them for every successive week, till the series be completed.

UNION OF THE "LONDON JOURNAL" AND
THE "PRINTING MACHINE"
WEDNESDAY, MAY 27, 1835

On Saturday, June 6, at Mr. Knight's, 22 Ludgate Street, by the speciallest of all licenses (and the most reasonable) to wit, their own, will be married the parties above-mentioned; after which, the happy couple will set off for all parts of the world, and pass four thousand nine hundred and sixty honeymoons, such being, by the most moderate computation, the term of their natural lives.

Yes, dear Reader, the LONDON JOURNAL is about to "change its condition:" — not itself, observe; for why should it? It will never be more itself than at this moment; as a married journal ought to be. It only changes, or rather enriches, its condition, its relative circumstances; and being a paper, it naturally marries a printing-machine; and its partner, being a machine of the most unmechanical and intelligent description, is to be very generous and amiable, and accommodate its humours to it in so charming a manner, that there would be an end of its having any will of its own, if the two wills did not thus become one, and merge will into pleasure. And thus what a happy pair shall we be; and how glad our ninety-nine thousand hosts will be to see us every Saturday morning, like some immortal and ubiquitous Monsieur and Madame Dacier, clubbing their stocks of scholarship, and presenting themselves in all those quarters at once, chatting and to chat, and with hands full of flowers, after the fashion of those groups on the old curtains, in which the same identical shepherd and shepherdess are reiterated through the whole district of chintz!

But marriage is expensive; and we are very much of the honest opinion of that custom in Wales, by which young couples are set up in life by the joint contributions of their friends, the favours to be returned on the like occasion; so, in a like beautiful spirit of reciprocity, we plainly tell our loving Readers, that they must assist us, and prepare themselves for a magnanimous rise in the estimation of our worth, to the value of One Halfpenny; – with this difference, however, from the Welsh state of the case, – that the benefit to be received from us in return is not prospective, but immediate, and that our halfpennyworth of increased attraction and entertainment will have evinced a modesty (not to mince the matter) astonishing, in rating its value so low. – To drop the metaphor, and state the case simply to the readers both of the LONDON JOURNAL and the PRINTING MACHINE, we would have them consider, that such as have already taken in both those papers, and therefore paid four-pence halfpenny for the two, may now have the essence of both for less than half the money, and that such as have only taken in one, may now have two instead of one, at the least possible increase of price in one case, and a great lowering of it in the other. The worth of each paper will be augmented, we conceive, by concentration, – none of the best matter of either being lost, and none of doubtful value being required in order to fill up; so that here will be the LONDON JOURNAL at its old price, with the PRINTING MACHINE added to it *for a halfpenny*; or the PRINTING MACHINE at two-thirds its old price with the LONDON JOURNAL added to it *for nothing*! It does not become us to deal in notes of admiration, and statements of our own merits; but we should like some eloquent third party, – Mr. Robins, for instance, – to have this matter to expatiate on, in some candid pulpit, or long and just advertisement. We fancy we see the TALL CAPITALS and BRILLIANT ADVANTAGES rearing their heads at intervals amidst the exuberant set-out, like the Pagoda in Kew Gardens, or the minarets of some Eastern paradise; and if he entered thoroughly into our merits, and did really set out the allurements of all our Gardens, fabulous and real, and of the stories told in them, and the great men beheld in them, and the light thrown by the sunbeams upon their minutest flowers and pebbles, we ask, with an emphatic but tranquil modesty, where *would* he stop? He would be obliged to have a whole "Times" or "Chronicle" to himself, – the news of the day coming in at the close of the last column, in a brief paragraph; – lamenting, that it can "barely allude to interesting intelligence from Paris," – "but the IMPORTANT ADVERTISEMENT" —

We *have* heard it whispered, we must confess, in one or two quarters, that there may be some possible peril in raising the price of our Journal, even so small a sum, considering how many new readers there are now-a-days, of such publications, struggling with unfitting poverty; but we have reason to doubt whether we have many readers so poor as the doubt supposes, whatever be the narrowness of means which they contrive to square with the demands of intellectual thirst and hunger; and readers of *that* kind we have no fear of losing. It has even happened to us, that Correspondents have advised us to raise our price, before we had any such grounds for it as at present; and an intelligent and long-established bookseller, who gave us the same advice, said "Depend upon it, that readers who take in such a paper as the LONDON JOURNAL, must like it for the liberal opinions it recommends, and are not the men to part company with it for a halfpenny."

The readers of the London Journal, all rising in a body, and speaking with a soul of loving indignation at the doubt. Believe him, sir; believe him.

Readers of the Printing Machine, rising also. And are we to be doubted? Has not the Printing Machine abounded in contempt of sordidness?

Here the Editor makes a bow to innumerable faces, right

and left of him; and endeavours to maintain a becoming aspect, between his natural indifference to pence, and his acquired sense of their value, and gratitude for regard.

In sober truth, we hope this junction of the two papers will be as acceptable to our friends, as it is pleasant to ourselves. The LONDON JOURNAL has long desired to be helped and enriched by other regular contributors. And in this case the Editor will be assisted in point of time, labour, and materials, not only by additional contributions, but by having a large and distinct portion of the united work placed under the responsible management of the gentleman who has edited the PRINTING MACHINE from its commencement. If the separate responsibilities were not so defined as they are in this instance, still we should have no apprehension of any collision of opinion. We are not strangers; and upon all the great principles by which the opinions and feelings of men are determined, we have as perfect an agreement as can be expected from those who hold the right of thinking for themselves, with the most hearty toleration of the thoughts of others. Nor will the Editor of THE LONDON JOURNAL omit a single contribution of his own; the old original articles, and the Romances of Real Life, Fine Arts, &c., will appear as usual, none the worse for an arrangement which may be of very serious benefit to himself; and as circumstances tend to show every day, that more good can be done to all parties by publications rather miscellaneous than critical, Mr. Knight gladly takes occasion of throwing one paper into the other, and the writers of the PRINTING MACHINE as gladly avail themselves of their briefer, and more concentrated columns, to confine their notices in future to books of the most interesting description exclusively, the nuts and sweetmeats of the tribe.

About five Pages will be devoted to the LONDON JOURNAL, and its usual variety of matter; about three to the review of books, constituting the PRINTING MACHINE. And if good spirits, plenty of subjects, and cordial co-operation, can do anything towards making our paper better than before, we confidently reckon upon its being so.

˙·˙ The Reader will observe that our day of publication is changed from Wednesday to Saturday. We confess we take leave of the old day with a pang, partly for old acquaintance sake (in the "Indicator" and "Tatler"), and partly because Charles Lamb (whose praise warrants us in being venturous enough to repeat it) said that the former of those publications made

"Wednesday the sweetest in the week."

(We are afraid we are guilty of a great piece of egotism here, but the recollection of the man must excuse it.) The reason however why we make the change is, that Saturday turns out to be the most convenient and profitable day for publication. Readers of cheap periodical papers, for the most part, find the close of the week the most convenient time for reading them, – making them part of their Sabbath recreation (let us add, no profane part, considering the uses and beauties of God's creation which they set forth) ; and the vendors of such papers, which are mostly published on the Saturday, crowd for them accordingly towards the close of the week, like people to a fair, and are apt, naturally enough, to look upon a call on their time and attention, on less customary days, as a supererogation which considerate editors might spare them. We propose, therefore, in future, to fall in with the crowd of comforts and conveniences at the end of the week, and become a part of its repose, and leisure, and contemplative enjoyment.

We hope we shall be thumbed horribly, and carried about in pockets, like a love-letter, or other certificate of merit.

THE SEER; OR, COMMON-PLACES REFRESHED

1840

PREFACE

The following Essays have been collected, for the first time, from such of the author's periodical writings as it was thought might furnish another publication similar to the *Indicator*. Most of them have been taken from the *London Journal*; and the remainder from the *Liberal*, the *Monthly Repository*, the *Tatler* and the *Round Table*. The title, of course, is to be understood in its primitive and most simple sense, and not in its portentous one, as connected with foresight and prophecy; nor would the author profess, intellectually, to see "farther into a mill-stone" than his betters. His motto, which thoroughly explains, will also, he trusts, vindicate all which he aspires to show; which is, that the more we look at anything in this beautiful and abundant world, with a desire to be pleased with it, the more we shall be rewarded by the loving spirit of the universe, with discoveries that await only the desire.

It will ever be one of the most delightful recollections of the author's life, that the periodical work, from which the collection has been chiefly made, was encouraged by all parties in the spirit in which it was set up. . . .

And so, with thanks and blessings upon the warm-hearted of all parties, who love their fellow-creatures quite as much as we do, perhaps better, and who may think, for that very reason, that the edge of their contest with one another is still not to be so much softened as we suppose, here is another bit of a corner, at all events, where, as in the recesses of their own minds, all green and hopeful thoughts for the good and entertainment of men may lovingly meet.

> [Given at our suburban abode, with a fire on one side of us, and a vine at the window on the other, this 19th day of October, one thousand eight hundred and forty, and in the very green and invincible year of our life, the fifty-sixth.]

L. H.

LEIGH HUNT'S JOURNAL

A MISCELLANY FOR THE CULTIVATION OF THE MEMORABLE, THE PROGRESSIVE, AND THE BEAUTIFUL

EDITOR'S ADDRESS TO THE READER

DECEMBER 7, 1850

HEALTH AND A HAPPY CHRISTMAS TO ALL OUR READERS! OLD AND NEW. To the old, for the sake of "Auld Lang Syne"; and to the new, whether old or young, in the hope that they may continue to be as young of heart; which is the reward, it seems, of such as remain constant to a certain kind of journalism.

Requested by my associates in this publication to give it the name which it bears, and thus, in a manner, personally reappearing as a journalist, it might be thought, perhaps, less modest than assured, if I entered abruptly on my task, and made no allusion to the circumstance. Kindest greetings, then, to all right good souls as aforesaid; and may I be half as welcome to them, as they will be to me!

I confess that I would rather not have had the title of the paper identified with my name; but the feeling which makes me do so, is, I fear, a sophistication or conventionalism, not worth attending to; one that, with so many good examples to warrant me, I ought to be ashamed of: and, accordingly, I am so. At all events, it is a trifle not worth saying more about. The object of the paper is another matter. There are great changes coming in the world; great modifications of the best things in it, and new leave-takings, I hope, of the worst. So thinks and hopes every body who thinks at all. So intimated Prince Albert to the citizens of London in the best speech ever made by a prince in this country; adding, that he "conceived it to be the duty of every educated person closely to watch and study the time in which he lives, and, as far as in him lies, to add his humble mite of individual exertion to further the accomplishment of what he believes Providence to have ordained."

Now the object which I have most at heart in the new Journal is to help in assisting the right progress of these changes, by the cultivation of a spirit of cheerfulness, reasonableness, and peace; and the most special means which I look for to this end, and which I earnestly desire on all sides, from all parties and shades of party, or of no party at all, is the countenance and co-operation of men the most distinguished for genius and public spirit. I hope they will deign to consider the Journal as a kind of neutral ground, or academic grove and resort of wit and philosophy, in which, while they freely express their opinions, whatever those may be, they will do so in accordance with the particular spirit of the place, and whether or not they think it the best and most useful spirit to be evinced at other times.

I could not give a better instance of what I mean, than by referring to the encouragement extended to my outset by my (in every sense of the word) great friend Thomas Carlyle, who, though I strongly differ with him respecting some other great men, and though I had but lately ventured some public remonstrances with his preference of that stormy to the sunny treatment of existing human affairs, which he thinks necessary to their well-being, has not only bid me God-speed in my undertaking in a manner the most practical and desirable, but answered those remonstrances in such beautiful private words, as I only wish delicacy could allow me to publish:

they are so full of that superiority to self-love, and that very honey of kindness and goodness, which lie at the core of all truly great hearts.

Such excellent things are sincerity and good intention in the highest minds, or in any minds. And so truly do they, and they only, enable a man to discern them in others, and to pardon them when differing with himself.

With respect to my own part in the Journal, it is the first time in my life that, in a work of this nature, I have had men of business at my side, who, in addition to their power of assisting in the literary portion, will give it those chances of circulation which can only be found in commercial channels. The tone and temper of the articles which I shall write, will be the same as in the Journal which had nearly the same title; and as to my opinions, they will be expressed so entirely with the usual freedom, that my readers will soon see whether I continue to deserve the good wishes of my friends the Many, or whether, and by which of their conflicting judgments, I am to be estimated according to certain of the Few; whether as a person who would pull down all religion and government; or whether as a person who would set all up; or whether as a person who would set them up this week, and pull them down the next; or, on the other hand, just *vice versa* to that (purely to oblige a gentleman who had a preconception to that effect). All this I shall thankfully leave to such trouble as the reader may choose to take on the subject; myself having got tired of autobiographical statements of any kind, especially to such differers with me in opinion as have made up their minds publicly on the subject, and who therefore cannot afford to undo those very important parcels. Some of these gentlemen come to the most extraordinary conclusions, owing to mean ideas which it would be a meanness to refute; others for similar reasons "best known to themselves;"

and some from sheer confusion of one person with another. It has always been so, and always will, as long as people are more uneasy at giving up a mistake than doing justice.

My late admirable friend Thomas Campbell, when I first knew him, was persuaded by one of them to take me for Henry Hunt, the pike-parader at Bristol. Not long since, Douglas Jerrold, of whom I never uttered a word, public or private, except in friendliness (due to him for his genius and his long friendship for myself), was told by another (who it was, I know not), that in something which I had said to the advantage of his wit and popularity, I intended, not to praise, but to abuse him! And a little before this, a friend in a manufacturing town was informed that I was a terrible speculator in the money markets! I, who was never in a market of any kind but to buy an apple or a flower, and who could not dabble in money dealings if I would, from sheer ignorance of their language.

But enough of enemies, for ever. Of friends, never. I confidently trust my undertaking in the hands of those, and of the public at large, feeling sure that they will not disapprove its spirit, whatever they may say to its power; and hoping that the distinguished correspondents who commence with it, and other younger and to-be-distinguished ones whom I expect in their company, will save it from falling off, should my own strength be insufficient. I feel no abatement of it yet, thank God, as far as brain, or as heart and hope are concerned; and success may give it me in respects less important.

The plan of the Journal will be seen from this first number; and so

"Chi lo leggerà, viva felice."
May he, and she, that read it, live and prosper.

LEIGH HUNT

CLASSIC TALES, Serious and Lively: With Critical Essays on the Merits and Reputations of the Authors. 5 vols. 1806-7

PREFACE

All nations have been delighted with fictitious story, for it suits all men. Real history, which exhibits the general events of the world, teaches us less real wisdom, for it seldom or never concerns us individually; it may instruct the warrior and the statesman, but we are not all warriors and statesmen; it may explain the art of managing empires, but, thank heaven, we are not all born to the management of empires: amidst all its instruction it teaches us little of the *human heart*, for those who make the greatest display in history are generally performing their parts in a mask; their actions are perfectly open to the world, but their hearts, if they have any, are mostly kept to themselves. It is for this reason that history is inferior to biography; the latter instructs us more particularly in the cause and origin of human actions: the knowledge of private life is the foundation of wisdom, that of public life is the superstructure: let us study ourselves first as *men*, and we may study ourselves afterwards as public characters.

But Biography is generally confined to the lives of those whose talents have rendered them conspicuous in the world; if we never hear of a man's existence from his own talents, we shall not easily be persuaded to hear of him by the talents of his biographer; and after all his biographer may know nothing of his subject, but what he gathers from his writings, his traditional sayings, or his parish register. Thus neither

History nor Biography can instruct us sufficiently in that class of mankind who compose the greatest part of what is called *the world*; yet it is as necessary to a complete knowledge of mankind to understand the little passions and adventures of private life, as it is to a complete botanist to understand the thorn that creeps through a hedge, or the nettle that hides itself in a ditch.

To supply this deficiency the instructors of mankind produced the Tale and the Novel, a species of literature which like all others has been abused, and abused most because it is most adapted to please us. The wisest of the ancients delivered their conceptions of the Deity and their lessons of morality in fables and parables; if the ignorant mistook their intentions, if they mistook the fable for the moral, and worshipped the vial that contained the truth for the pure essence within, it argues nothing but their own folly; if in our own times, the Tales of celebrated novelists have been wretchedly copied by those who could not apply them to human life, it argues nothing but the ignorance of the copyists: *such writers* we shall gladly let alone: we do not wish to disturb them in their *marble-covered monuments*; we shall attend rather to the living dead than to the dead living. In short, our title page, if it speaks the truth, will speak best for our intentions: we will not hazard the incredulity of our readers by promising much; perhaps we shall perform but little, but at any rate we shall act with caution, and with our best taste, and our little may probably be good. Let us not be deceived by names; the titles of Biographer and Historian are nobler sounds than those of Novelist and Writer of Tales, but let it be recollected that there is more real wisdom in the Fables of Æsop than in all the Histories of Europe put together.

L. H.

A BOOK FOR A CORNER; or Selections in Prose and Verse. 2 vols. 1849

PREFACE

An ample account of the nature of this work will be found in the *Introduction*; but to give a brief and more general idea of the entertainment which it is proposed to set before the purchaser, it may be as well to state in this place, that the book, for the most part, is a collection of passages from such authors as retain, if not the highest, yet the most friendly and as it were domestic hold upon us during life, and sympathize with us through all portions of it. Hence the first extract is a Letter addressed to an Infant, the last the Elegy in the Churchyard, and the intermediate ones have something of an analogous reference to the successive stages of existence. It is therefore intended to be read by intelligent persons of all times of life, the youthful associations in it being such as the oldest readers love to call to mind, and the oldest such as all would gladly meet with in their decline. It has no politics in it, no polemics, nothing to offend the delicatest mind. The innocentest boy and the most cautious of his seniors might alike be glad to look over the other's shoulder, and find him in his corner perusing it.

This may be speaking in a boastful manner; but an Editor has a right to boast of his originals, especially when they are such as have comforted and delighted him throughout his own life, and are for that reason recommended by him to others.

He would also claim for it a merit, great in the wise eyes of children, and becoming greater every day in those of the community at large; namely, that of its being a Book of Pictures. If he had had the pleasure of having the artist at his elbow, he might have requested him to make a little change in two or three instances, such as omitting the bird-cage on the old lady's table, and making the approach to his Castle of Indolence a little more easy; but he has enjoyed his landscapes and his domesticities, has walked with great satisfaction in his bowery places, and returns him special thanks for the abode of the Schoolmistress.

A BOOK FOR A CORNER

NATURE OF THE PRESENT WORK, AND A FEW REMARKS ON ITS READERS

This compilation is intended for all lovers of books, at every time of life, from childhood to old age, particularly such as are fond of the authors it quotes, and who enjoy their perusal most in the quietest places. It is intended for the boy or girl who loves to get with a book into a corner – for the youth who on entering life finds his advantage in having become acquainted with books – for the man in the thick of life, to whose spare moments books are refreshments – and for persons in the decline of life, who reflect on what they have experienced, and to whom books and gardens afford their tranquillest pleasures.

It is a book (not to say it immodestly) intended to lie in old parlour windows, in studies, in cottages, in cabins aboard ship, in country-inns, in country-houses, in summer-houses, in any houses that have wit enough to like it, and are not the mere victims of a table covered with books for show.

When Shenstone was a child, he used to have a new book brought him from the next country-town, whenever any body went to market. If he had gone to bed and was asleep, it was put behind his pillow; and if it had been forgotten, and he was awake, his mother (more kindly than wisely) "wrapped up a piece of wood of the same form, and pacified him for the night." This is the sort of child we hope to be a reader of our volumes.

When Gray and Walpole were at Eton, they partitioned out the fields into territories of which they had read in books, and so ruled over them and sent ambassadors to one another. These are the sort of school-boys we look to entertain.

When Mrs. Inchbald, who was a farmer's daughter, first came to London, she was alone, and would have been subjected to no small perils but for the knowledge she had acquired from books; for she was poor, lovely, and sensitive. She turned the knowledge to the greatest account, and lived to add precious matter to the stock. We flatter ourselves, or rather we dare to aver, considering the authors who furnish our extracts, that nobody would have more approved of our book than Mrs. Inchbald.

Some of the most stirring men in the world, persons in the thick of business of all kinds, and indeed with the business of the world itself on their hands, — Lorenzo de Medici, for instance, who was at once the great merchant and the political arbiter of his time, — have combined with their other energies the greatest love of books, and found no recreation at once so wholesome and so useful. We hope many a man of business will refresh himself with the short pieces in these volumes, and return to his work the fitter to baffle craft, and yet retain a reverence for simplicity.

Every man who has a right sense of business, whether his business be that of the world or of himself, has a respect for all right things apart from it; because business with him is not a mindless and merely instinctive industry, like that of a beetle rolling its ball of clay, but an exercise of faculties congenial with the other powers of the human being, and all working to some social end. Hence he approves of judicious and refreshing leisure – of domestic and social evenings – of suburban retreats – of gardens – of ultimate retirement "for good" – of a reading and reflective old age. Such retirements have been longed for, and in many instances realized, by wise and great men of all classes, from the Diocletians of old to the Foxes and Burkes of our own days. Warren Hastings, who had ruled India, yearned for the scenes of his boyhood; and lived to be happy in them. The wish to possess a country-house, a retreat, a nest, a harbour of some kind from the storms and even from the agitating pleasures of life, is as old as the sorrows and joys of civilization. The child feels it when he "plays at house"; the schoolboy, when he is reading in his corner; the lover, when he thinks of his mistress. Epicurus felt it in his garden; Horace and Virgil expressed their desire of it in passages which the sympathy of mankind has rendered immortal. It was the end of all the wisdom and experience of Shakspeare. He retired to his native town, and built himself a house in which he died. And who else does not occasionally "flit" somewhere meantime if he can? The country for many miles round London, and indeed in most other places, is adorned with houses and grounds of men of business, who are whirled to and fro on weekly or daily evenings, and who would all find something to approve in the closing chapters of our work. The greatest monied man of our time, Roths-child, who weighed kings in his balance, could not do without his house at Gunnersbury. Even the turbulent De Retz, ac-cording to Madame de Sévigné, became the sweetest of re-tired Signiors, and did nothing but read books and feed his trout. It is customary to jest upon such men, and indeed upon all retirement; to say that they would still meddle with af-fairs if they could, and that retirement is a failure and a "bore." Fox did not think so. It is possible that De Retz would have meddled fast enough; nor are many energetic men superior, perhaps, to temptations of their spirit in this

way, when such occur. But this does not hinder them from
enjoying another and a seasonable pleasure meantime. On the
contrary, this very energy is the thing which hinders it from
palling; that is to say, supposing their intellects are large
enough to include a sense of it. De Retz, like Burke and Fox,
was a lover of books. Sir Robert Walpole, who retired only
to be sick and to die, did not care for books. Occupation is
the necessary basis of all enjoyment; and he who cannot read,
or botanize, or farm, or amuse himself with his neighbours,
or exercise his brain with thinking, is in a bad way for the
country at any time, much more for retiring into it. He has
nothing to do but to get back as fast as he can, and be hustled
into a sensation by a mob.

"Books, Venus, books." It is those that teach us to refine on
our pleasures when young, and which, having so taught us,
enable us to recall them with satisfaction when old. For let
the half-witted say what they will of delusions, no thorough
reader ever ceased to believe in his books, whatever doubts
they might have taught him by the way. They are pleasures
too palpable and habitual for him to deny. The habit itself is
a pleasure. They contain his young dreams and his old discoveries; all that he has lost, as well as all that he has gained;
and, as he is no surer of the gain than of the loss, except in
proportion to the strength of his perceptions, the dreams, in
being renewed, become truths again. He is again in commun-
ion with the past; again interested in its adventures, grieving
with its griefs, laughing with its merriment, forgetting the
very chair and room he is sitting in. Who, in the mysterious
operation of things, shall dare to assert in what unreal corner
of time and space that man's mind is; or what better proof
he has of the existence of the poor goods and chattels about
him, which at that moment (to him) are non-existent? "Oh!"
people say, "but he wakes up, and sees them there." Well; he
woke *down* then, and saw the rest. What we distinguish into

dreams and realities, are, in both cases, but representatives of impressions. Who shall know what difference there is in them at all, save that of degree, till some higher state of existence help us to a criterion?

For our part, such real things to us are books, that, if habit and perception make the difference between real and unreal, we may say that we more frequently wake out of common life to *them*, than out of them to common life. Yet we do not find the life the less real. We only feel books to be a constituent part of it; a world, as the poet says,

> Round which, with tendrils strong as flesh and blood,
> Our pastime and our happiness may grow.

What do readers care for "existing things" (except when Ireland is mentioned, or a child is grieving) compared with poetry and romance? What for Bonaparte and his pretences, compared with the honest jealousy of "Orlando," or the cakes of Alfred? What for all the parsons in the world (except Pius IX. or some Welsh curate) compared with Parson Adams or the Vicar of Wakefield? What men (generally speaking) are they so sure of? are so intimate with? can describe, quote, and talk of to one another with so much certainty of a mutual interest? And yet, when readers wake up to that other dream of life, called real life (and we do not mean to deny its palpability), they do not find their enjoyment of it diminished. It is increased – increased by the contrast – by the variety – by the call upon them to show the faith which books have originally given them in all true and good things, and which books, in spite of contradiction and disappointment, have constantly maintained. Mankind are the creatures of books, as well as of other circumstances; and such they eternally remain; proofs, that the race is a noble and a believing race, and capable of whatever books can stimulate.

The volumes now offered to our fellow readers originated
in this kind of passion for books. They were suggested by a
wish we had long felt to get up a book for our private enjoyment, and of a very particular and unambitious nature. It
was to have consisted of favourite passages, not out of the
authors we most admired, but those whom we most loved;
and it was to have commenced, as the volumes do, with Shenstone's *Schoolmistress*, and ended with Gray's *Elegy*. It was
to have contained indeed little which the volumes do not comprise, though not intended to be half so big, and it was to
have proceeded on the same plan of beginning with childhood
and ending with the church-yard. We did not intend to omit
the greatest authors on account of their being the greatest,
but because they moved the feelings too strongly. What we
desired was not an excitement, but a balm. Readers, who have
led stirring lives, have such men as Shakspeare with them
always, in their very struggles and sufferings, and in the
tragic spectacles of the world. Great crowds and great passions are Shakspeares; and we, for one (and such we take to
be the case with many readers), are sometimes as willing to
retire from their "infinite agitation of wit," as from strifes
less exalted; and retreat into the placider corners of genius
more humble. It is out of no disrespect to their greatness;
neither, we may be allowed to say, is it from any fear of being unable to sustain it; for we have seen perhaps as many
appalling faces of things in our time as they have, and we are
always ready to confront more if duty demand it. But we do
not choose to be always suffering over again in books what we
have suffered in the world. We prefer, when in a state of
repose, to renew what we have enjoyed – to possess wholly
what we enjoy still – to discern in the least and gentlest
things the greatest and sweetest intentions of Nature – and to
cultivate those soothing, serene, and affectionate feelings,
which leave us in peace with all the world, and in good hope

of the world to come. The very greatest genius, after all, is not the greatest thing in the world, any more than the greatest city in the world is the country or the sky. It is a concentration of some of its greatest powers, but it is not the greatest diffusion of its might. It is not the habit of its success, the stability of its sereness. And this is what readers like ourselves desire to feel and know. The greatest use of genius is but to subserve to that end; to further the means of enjoying it, and to freshen and keep it pure; as the winds and thunders, which come rarely, are purifiers of the sweet fields, which are abiding.

The book, therefore, as originally contemplated, was to consist principally, besides the pieces mentioned, of such others as Cowley's *Garden*, Wotten's *Happy Life*, the favourite passages about the country from Horace and Virgil, Claudian's *Old Man of Verona*, Pope's *Ode on Solitude*, a selection from the Coverley papers in the *Spectator*, Thomson's *Castle of Indolence, Letters* of Gray, Virgil's *Gnat* out of Spenser; and, though we have several editions of the work constantly by us, we think we could not have denied ourselves the pleasure of having something out of the *Arabian Nights*. Our *Sequestered Book* (for such, in our mind, we called it) would hardly have seemed complete without a chapter or two about *Sindbad* or the *Forty Thieves*, or the retirement of the *Fairy Banou*. The book was to have been addressed entirely to lovers of sequestered pleasures, and chiefly to such as were in the decline of life, or poetically beginning it.

When the volume, however, came to be considered with a view to publication, objections were made to the smallness of its size, and the probable fewness of its readers. Had we been rich, we should have parried the objection, and sent forth a volume at any rate, with the contents of which the few would have been pleased. We consoled ourselves with reflecting that we had other favourite passages which could be included in a larger book; and an extension of the plan now struck us, which in the eyes of many readers, perhaps of most, would in all probability improve it. This was, to suppose our sequestered reader thinking, not merely of the pleasures of his childhood or of his old age, but of his whole life, past or to come, and thus calling to mind passages from favourite authors of all kinds in illustration of its successive phases. The spirit of the first conception was still, however, to be carefully retained. Life, without effeminately shutting one's eyes to its perplexities, was to be regarded, not in spleen, or in sorrow, or in narrowness of any kind, but with a cheerfulness befitting childhood, a manliness befitting a man, and with that calm and loving wisdom in age which discerns so much beauty and goodness in the face of Nature, that it cannot doubt the benevolence of her soul.

Hence the inclusion in the present volume of knaveries and other half-witted activities out in the world, and of terrors and tragedies in solitude. Hence extracts from Le Sage and Fielding, from Steele, Smollett, Goldsmith, Mrs. Radcliffe, and others.

We have imagined a book-loving man, or man able to refresh himself with books, at every successive period of his life; – the child at his primer, the sanguine boy, the youth entering the world, the man in the thick of it, the man of alternate business and repose, the retired man calmly considering his birth and his death; and in this one human being we include, of course, the whole race and both sexes, mothers, wives, and daughters, and all which they do to animate and sweeten existence. Thus our invisible, or rather many-bodied hero (who is the reader himself), is in the first instance a baby; then a child under the *Schoolmistress* of Shenstone; then the schoolboy with Gray and Walpole, reading poetry and romance; then *Gil Blas* entering the world; then the sympathiser with the *John Buncles* who enjoy it, and the *Travellers* who fill it with enterprise; then the matured man beginning to talk of disappointments, and standing in need of admonition *Against Inconsistency in his Expectations*; then the reassured man comforted by his honesty and his just hopes, and refreshing himself with his *Club* or his country-lodging, his pictures, or his theatre; then the retiring, or retired, or finally old man, looking back with tenderness on his enjoyments, with regret for his errors, with comfort in his virtues, and with a charity for all men, which gives him a right to the comfort; loving all the good things he ever loved, particularly the books which have been his companions and the childhood which he meets again in the fields; and neither wishing nor fearing to be gathered into that kindly bosom of Nature, which covers the fields with flowers, and is encircled with the heavens.

The reader, however, is not to suppose that any attention to this plan of the book is exacted of him. Such a demand would be a pedantry and a folly. It is only suggested to him in case he may like it, and for the purpose of showing that we set nothing before him which does not possess a principle of order. He may regard the book, if more convenient to do so, as a mere set of extracts with comments, or of extracts alone, not requiring comments. Our sequestered book was to have been without comments; and we should have been well content, had none been desired for this. There is a pleasure, it is true, in expressing love and admiration, and in hoping that we contribute to the extension of such feelings in the world; but we can truly say, that we seldom quote a fine passage, and comment upon it at any length, without wishing that everybody had been as well acquainted with it as ourselves, and could dispense with the recommendation. All we expect of the reader is that he should like the extracts on which the comments are made. If he does not do that, he has no business to be a reader of the book, or perhaps to be a reader at all. At least he is no universalist; no sympathiser with the entire and genial round of existence; and it is for the reader who is, that these volumes are emphatically intended.

A universalist, in one high bibliographical respect, may be said to be the only true reader; for he is the only reader on whom no writing is lost. Too many people approve no books but such as are representatives of some opinion or passion of their own. They read, not to have human nature reflected on them, and so be taught to know and to love everything, but to be reflected themselves as in a pocket mirror, and so interchange admiring looks with their own narrow cast of countenance. The universalist alone puts up with difference of opinion, by reason of his own very difference; because his difference is a right claimed by him in the spirit of universal allowance, and not a privilege arrogated by conceit. He loves poetry and prose, fiction and matter of fact, seriousness and mirth, because he is a thorough human being, and contains portions of all the faculties to which they appeal. A man who can be nothing but serious, or nothing but merry, is but half a man. The lachrymal or the risible organs are wanting in him. He has no business to have eyes or muscles like other men. The universalist alone can put up with *him*, by reason of the very sympathy of his antipathy. He understands the defect enough to pity, while he dislikes it. The universalist is the only reader who can make something out of books for which he has no predilection. He sees differences in them to sharpen his reasoning; sciences which impress on him a sense of his ignorance; nay, languages which, if they can do nothing else, amuse his eye and set him thinking of other countries. He will detect old acquaintances in Arabic numerals, and puzzle over a sum or a problem, if only to try and taste the curiosity of it. He is the only man (except a soldier or a gardener) to whom an army list or an almanac would not be thoroughly disgusting on a rainy day in a country ale-house, when nothing else readable is at hand, and the coach has gone "just ten minutes." The zodiacal light of "Francis Moore, Physician," would not be lost on him. He would laugh at the Doctor's verses; wonder who St. Alphage or St. Hugh could have been, as affecting the red-letter days; and see what christian or surnames prevailed in the army, or what personages had authority in those days. The words "Royal Highness the Duke of York" would set him thinking on that good-natured though not astonishing prince, and imagining how hearty a dish of beef-steaks he would have dispatched in the room in which he was sitting.

Our compilation, therefore, though desirous to please all who are willing to be pleased, is ambitious to satisfy this sort of person most of all. It is of *his* childhood we were mostly thinking when we extracted the *Schoolmistress*. He will thoroughly understand the wisdom lurking beneath the playfulness of its author. *He* will know how wholesome as well as amusing it is to become acquainted with books like *Gil Blas* and *Joseph Andrews*. *He* will derive agreeable terror from *Sir Bertram* and the *Haunted Chamber*; will assent with delighted reason to every sentence in *Mrs. Barbauld's Essay*; will feel himself wandering into solitudes with *Gray*; shake honest hands with *Sir Roger de Coverley*; be ready to embrace *Parson Adams*, and to chuck *Pounce* out of window, instead of the hat; will travel with *Marco Polo* and *Mungo Park*; stay at home with *Thomson*; retire with *Cowley*; be industrious with *Hutton*; sympathizing with *Gay* and *Mrs. Inchbald*; laughing with (and at) *Buncle*; melancholy and forlorn, and self-restored, with the shipwrecked mariner of *De Foe*. There are *Robinson Crusoes* in the moral as well as physical world, and even a universalist may be one of them; — men, cast on desert islands of thought and speculation; without companionship; without worldly resources;

forced to arm and clothe themselves out of the remains of
shipwrecked hopes, and to make a home for their solitary
hearts in the nooks and corners of imagination and reading.
It is not the worst lot in the world. Turned to account for
others, and embraced with patient cheerfulness, it may, with
few exceptions, even be one of the best. We hope our volume
may light into the hands of such men. Every extract which is
made in it, has something of a like second-purpose, beyond
what appears on its face. There is amusement for those who
require nothing more, and instruction in the shape of amusement for those who choose to find it. We only hope that the
"knowing reader" will not think we have assisted inquiry too
often. We hate, with our friends the little boys, nothing so
much as the "Moral" that officiously treads the heels of the
great Æsop, and which assumes that the sage has not done his
work when he has told his story. It is bad enough to be forced
to interpret wisdom of any kind; but to talk after such trans-
parent lessons as those, is overweeningness horrible. The little
boys will find nothing of the sort to frighten them in this
book; and they need not look at the prefaces, if they have no
mind for them. It is beautiful to think how ignorant our
grown memories are of prefaces to books of amusement that
were put into our hands when young, and how intensely we
remember the best extracts. What grown-up people in general
know anything of good Dr. Enfield or didactic Dr. Knox, or
even of Percy, the editor of *Ancient Reliques*? Yet who that
has read the *Speaker* and *Elegant Extracts* ever forgot the
soliloquy in *Hamlet*, Goldsmith's *Beau Tibbs* and *Contented
Beggar*, or the story of *Robin Hood*?

Those exquisite humours of Goldsmith, and the story of
Robin Hood, we have omitted, with a hundred others, partly
because we had not room for an abundance of things which
we admired, chiefly because they did not fall within a certain
idea of our plan. The extremely familiar knowledge also

which readers have of them might have been another objection, even in a work consisting chiefly of favourite passages;—things, which imply a certain amount of familiar knowledge, if not in the public at large, yet among readers in general. If any persons should object that some of these also are too familiar, the answer is, that they are of a nature which rendered it impossible for us, consistently with our plan, to omit them, and that readers in general would have missed them. We allude, in particular, to the *Elegy in a Country Churchyard* and the *Ode on the Prospect of Eton College*. It is the privilege of fine writers, when happy in their treatment of a universal subject of thought or feeling, to leave such an impression of it in the reading world as almost to identify it with everybody's own reflections, or constitute it a sort of involuntary mental quotation. Of this kind are Gray's reflections in the church-yard, and his memories of school-boy happiness. Few people who know these passages by heart, ever think of a church-yard or a school-ground without calling them to mind.

The nature and the amount of the reader's familiarity with many other extracts are the reasons why we have extracted them. They constitute part of the object and essence of the book; for the familiarity is not a vulgar and repulsive one, but that of a noble and ever-fresh companion, whose society we can the less dispense with, the more we are accustomed to it. The book in this respect resembles a set of pictures which it delights us to live with, or a collection of favourite songs and pieces of music, which we bind up in volumes in order that we may always have them at hand, or know where to find them. Who, in such a room full of pictures, would object to his Raphael or Titian? Or in such a collection of music, to his Beethoven, Rossini, or Paisiello? Our book may have little novelty in the least sense of the word; but it has the best in the greatest sense; that is to say, *never-dying novelty*;

— antiquity hung with ivy-blossoms and rose-buds; old friends with the ever-new faces of wit, thought, and affection. Time has proved the genius with which it is filled. "Age cannot wither it," nor "custom stale its variety." We ourselves have read, and shall continue to read it to our dying day; and we should not say thus much, especially on such an occasion, if we did not know, that hundreds and thousands would do the same, whether they read it in this collection or not.

READINGS FOR RAILWAYS;
or, Anecdotes and other Short Stories.   [1850]

PREFACE

It seems not a little extraordinary, that among the books which are recommended by their publishers to railway perusal, or which have been expressly designed for that purpose by their authors, there does not appear to be a single volume of the present description. They are, all of them, (as far as I am aware), either reprints of novels, and other works of general literature, which might as well be read any where else; or scientific, statistical, or topographical accounts of railways themselves; which however interesting to the subscriber, the mechanician, or the lover of the country (and they are often extremely so), go to the other extreme of the novels, etc., and tend to keep the mind too exclusively fixed upon the railway itself; so that the noise of it may be said to be always ringing in the ear.

It has struck me, therefore, that a volume consisting of briefer passages on *all* subjects, not excluding the railway, but principally furnishing interest and amusement to any mood of mind, grave or gay, in which the traveller might happen to find himself, would be no unwelcome addition to the stock of the journeying public. They are of great variety as the title-page will have shown; some of them so brief, as to be readable in a minute, none of them demanding any tiresome length of attention; and not one, I will venture to say, without some kind of worth; for it was that, and that only which induced me to mark them for extract. Most of them, indeed, were marked solely for my own pleasure, in the course of a habit of that kind, in which I have ever indulged; and I thus offer to nobody a book which has not given entertainment and instruction to myself.

May it help to give as much zest to their pleasant moments, and solace to their anxious ones, as it has done to those of the compiler, serving to shorten the very speed of the railway itself, and to set them all down in good humour at their respective abodes. . . .

LEIGH HUNT

Kensington,
Dec. 1st, 1849.